CHOICES
of LOVE

CHOICES
OF LOVE

⌘

Dorothy Maclean

LINDISFARNE BOOKS

© Copyright 1998 Dorothy Maclean

Published by Lindisfarne Books
3390 Route 9, Hudson, NY 12534

Library of Congress Cataloging-in-Publication Data

Maclean, Dorothy.
    Choices of Love / Dorothy Maclean.
         p. cm.
    Includes bibliographical references
    ISBN 0-940262-90-8
    1. Maclean, Dorothy. 2. Spirits. 3. Spiritual life.
    4. Love-Religious aspects. 5. Findhorn Community—Biography.
    6. Occultists—Biography.   I. Title.
    BF1408.2.M32A3 1998
    131—dc21   98-5096
                                           CIP

Cover painting, *The Golden Cell* by Odilon Redon, © The British Museum.

10 9 8 7 6 5 4 3 2 1

Printed in the United States of America

CONTENTS

Dedicated to my fellow seekers

Acknowledgments

Many thanks to all the people who have supported and encouraged me to get on with this book and who have given me specific help. Among them are Margaret Carney, Erica Moore, Freya Secrest, Brian Ziegler, Bob Wright, Pam Williams, Gordon Cutler, Hiro McIlwraith, David and Ruth Ann Getchell, Ron Rabin, Al and Linda Souma, and Christopher Bamford. Thanks to May Hanna. Thanks to my editors, Jan Johnson and Marcia Merryman Means, for bringing in much-needed mental clarity. Thanks to David and Julie Spangler, who always expand my mind and delight my soul.

INTRODUCTION

MY BOOK *To Hear the Angels Sing*, written more than fifteen years ago, gives my perspective on the early days of the Findhorn Foundation. It tells how a community developed out of the commitment of three people—Eileen and Peter Caddy and me—to do what we called God's will. Each of us had experiences of the sacred and attempted to live according to inner guidance. We did not intend to start a community. It grew out of the development of the garden, and the garden grew out of the development of our cooperation with the inner essence of nature. The nature aspect was my particular contribution, leading to my experiencing the essence of not only the plant kingdom but of minerals, animals, and groups of human beings as well.

We found that inner contact was relevant at all levels of our lives, and the brilliant and unusual garden growth was the practical evidence. Speaking for myself, when I followed constant inner reminders to do everything with love, I felt better, things worked out, relationships with others improved. I have experienced many examples of the practicality of choosing love or connecting with the soul level and of how the results of these choices changed my life. For instance, I used to hate to live in cities, but I changed into a person who no longer has any problem in this respect, and that alone has had a huge influence on my life. It was contact with the angel of a city that made the difference in me.

In talking about God, which to me is the life force within everything, I use various words such as the Beloved, the sacred, wholeness, oneness, love, the presence. The dimensions of soul, the part of us and of everything that is closest in consciousness to inner divinity, I simply call the soul or angelic level. In these dimensions are the energies, the formless force fields that I name angels or devas. To me, the soul of anything, say a country, is basically the same as its angel. At the same time, everything that is external, being part of God, is also sacred.

Part one of the book deals with my connection to the sacred. All the wonderful experiences that have clarified my being have stemmed from "listening" to my inner knowing, to God the Beloved. Through the years I have found that people are open to finding enlightenment from many outer sources or from out-of-this-world sources, such as guides or space beings, but somehow they are not as open to seeking their inner wisdom. Our religious backgrounds have blocked our minds from gaining access to the one source that is behind all life. So I have started by delving more deeply into the marvelous care and training that I have received and that all of us receive when we turn to that source. For years I chose to begin the day by attuning to and wrapping myself in that great love that is at the core of us all. Gradually, through the years, my very personality became more loving, more amenable. I was learning from within that all situations are helped by love, that following such inward requests from God as "Wash the dishes with me" made my work and myself much more efficient and enjoyable. Then, when asked by God to attune to the essence of nature, I discovered other aspects of the wondrous life on this planet and realized that angels are the expression of and agents for creation that the Beloved works through.

Like most of us, I am interested in the question of good and evil. When I communicated with angels of qualities like serenity, I found them to be above polarity; the Angel of Joy and the Angel of Sorrow were one and the same angel. This knowledge helped direct me to explore the subject of evil more fully, and chapter two describes my searchings. Contact with the angels also revealed that soul qualities are intelligent energies in themselves and that each of them is an aspect of love. Through them I was led to understand a little of the creative process on Earth and the parts played by the four elements. These subjects may seem somewhat abstract, yet understanding them has been illuminating and helpful in my everyday life.

In part two, I share experiences resulting from soul contact with various parts of creation. The emphasis is on how we connect with other life on the planet and how we can use our creativity for the whole. As we link with different aspects of ourselves and the planet, we change ourselves *and* the planet. We have the capability of consciously connecting and cooperating with all life species. We can even consciously connect and cooperate with the souls of such human groups as cities and countries. It was through my connection with the soul of my native country of Canada that I recognized and began to free myself from the cultural biases that not only separated me from others but also caused me to act unconsciously. At the same time accepting and honoring my background was an essential basis for understanding my identity. Other experiences taught me more about the psychic level of consciousness and our ability to connect with and heal the mental and emotional projections we have created.

Often people have said to me that they can't communicate with God or with angels, or have asked me how to know what they are connecting with. One answer is that whether we are conscious of it or not, we are always attuning to these energies, for our core is a divine spark and our soul functions in the same realm as the angels. We have angelic qualities. If we had no connection with divinity, we would not be alive. However, most of us do not tend to feel very angelic or even want to! We have a divine essence, and we might as well admit it and live with it, for it is not going to go away. When we feel elements of wholeness, lightness, uplift, nonjudgment, or joy, we know we are in contact with the sacred. Conversely, if in our attunement we feel criticism, condemnation, or blame, we can know we are connecting to personal beliefs or prejudices that divide us from others.

A state of meditation is one way to make the inner connection, as suggested in the exercises given at the end of each chapter. Meditation can be the start of a deep communication and sharing with many realms within ourselves and others, and an aid to becoming more loving.

This book is about recognizing and realizing the transforming power of love, love not as the mushy sentiment that many believe it to be, but as the great source and power behind all life. Love is within all of us, open to all of us, often untapped because our civilization gives it little true credence. To honor and share that amazing love and wisdom is my great desire, and it is ultimately the destiny and joy of each one of us.

⌘ PART 1

CHAPTER ONE

THE BELOVED

ON THIS PLANET, the marvelous, cooperating, multiform worlds of nature also include our complex human natures with our known senses of touch, smell, taste, hearing, and sight, as well as our intangible senses. All these senses affect our bodies, emotions, minds, and souls. Through them we interact with the vast variety and beauty of creation. Some say it was by chance that all life appeared. Others believe that an intelligence must be present.

The great, mysterious influence responsible for and living within creation and holding it alive I call God the Beloved. We humans love naming things, but we find no adequate symbol or imagery sufficient to embrace this concept. It is just a concept to many, and to others it is an experience. Whatever we believe, the very fact of our existence, the fact that we are conscious, is utterly amazing. That we continue to have the power of choice, however irresponsible we are, implies a love huge enough to be eternal. Whatever we believe, there is something within us that longs for love. We want to be loved, and by the Beloved we are loved, though we may not know it.

We are all searching for something. The form of the search may change, particularly when we realize a goal. Another vision, another goal emerges. It may be a material possession or

position, or an inner attribute like power or ridding ourselves
of a quality that we dislike. We are never satisfied; we have
within us that which has been called "divine discontent." It
lives in us until in a moment of grace we are truly fulfilled. We
tap into an inexplicable vastness beyond thought and are integrated into a universal lovingness and knowingness. We find
love, and our world is forever changed.

To me, the Beloved is that eternal, complete love. A joy.
Omnipresent, omnipotent, omniscient—and fun. The darkness
and the light, the atom and the universe, the leaf and the storm,
beauty itself. The creator who shares creativeness. I could doubt-
less continue enumerating, for there is nowhere the sacred is not
present, and my concept of it expands as I experience more of
life. When I feel low, I lose touch with the reality of these definitions, but I somehow know that it is still there, always.

Views of the Sacred

There have been various attempts to define the Beloved. An
intelligible sphere whose center is everywhere and circumfer-
ence nowhere is one definition that made a certain sense to me.
I also accepted it as the ultimate principle, a cosmic process
that we try to evaluate through a small spectrum of frequencies.
When I recently attended a typical Christian church service, I
was appalled to hear the Beloved still referred to as a sort of
heavenly, punitive Man-Being "out there" somewhere. Since I
have always rejected the "man on a cloud" image and have long
accepted the reality of God within, the transcendent mystery
immanent in humans and all things, I had almost forgotten
that our culture paints such a limited, unempowering, and artificial picture of the Divine or that, for many, God is dead. I like
better a definition of God as the power of love holding the universe together.

The myths of almost all countries throughout history tell of a God or gods that give meaning and purpose to human life. Such concepts have been so powerful that civilizations have been built on them, and countless wars have been fought over their interpretation. Until recently in the West, the idea of God was the stabilizing and motivating force for life and an inspiration for the arts. Then, in the age of reason and Newtonian physics, this concept was replaced by one of clockwork action, of mechanical laws in a material universe. Science and technology in the twentieth century have evolved beyond the Newtonian world by discoveries in physics and cosmology, and the new story of science tells of fresh and expanded perspectives.

Personal Views

I did not always view God as love. My first ideas came from the Presbyterian Church of Canada Sunday school and church services I attended. Like any child, I imbibed my cultural background, taking it for granted without deriving any particular meaning. In my later teen years I discarded Christianity because I thought it did not answer my questions or satisfy my needs. It was peripheral to what unfolded for me in my ongoing inquiries. I was interested in and searched for answers to the whys and wherefores of existence, without finding solutions.

A step in my search came when I attended a Sufi Service of Universal Worship, during which all religions were honored as acceptable paths to God. This approach was one that resonated with me, and I joined the Sufi Order. The teachings of Hazrat Inayat Khan were simple, yet profound, and I eagerly read of them in books of his lectures. He began his talks with the phrase "Beloved ones of God," and Love, Harmony, and Beauty were his themes. From the reverence his living disciples gave him (he died when I was six), I thought that he was too good to be true and for years tried to find fault. But his personality seemed as benign as his teachings. This helped me realize that in this day and age there were people who truly followed spirit as Jesus did and who could be called "Christed" beings, a concept new to me. I had vivid dreams of Inayat Khan. In one I was a child covered with burrs; he picked me up, put me on his knees, and stroked me until all my burrs disappeared. His love for God helped me develop the notion of God as a more benevolent and accessible presence.

Then, in London, I again met the person who had chaperoned me on my trip from Toronto to New York, when I was starting my first job outside my native country. Sheena was a Scottish Quaker, seven years my senior and very beautiful. She gradually took on the role of teacher for me and other friends as we came to know and appreciate her helpfulness and the depth of her love. The child of missionary parents, even in her youth she considered doing God's will of paramount importance to her. God was love, and I Corinthians, chapter 13, was her favorite quotation, with "love" substituted for "charity." "Though I speak with the tongues of men and of angels, and have not love, I become as sounding brass, or a tinkling cymbal."

She was especially helpful in the ordinary circumstances of daily living, for to her everything was to be done with love. I remember that I used to lend her a hand by dusting her flat, a task I thoroughly disliked when I could see no dust, as was almost always the case. It all seemed a waste of time and energy. But I dutifully dusted, until one day she gently asked me to leave and not come back. The energy I was creating, she explained, was injurious to her and to her flat. I felt very exposed and ashamed, but the experience helped me learn that the attitude of being loving is more important than physical acts.

Through the years I would see a great deal of Sheena, and then experience periods without her. Gradually we became closer, and to a small group she began to give specific teachings based on her own inner attunement. I became her scribe, taking her talks down in shorthand and transcribing them. The mystical experience was real to her, and she did all she could to honor that loving reality in her life and help us do likewise.

The Mystical Experience

Mystics are people who experience a union with the divine. Their common message is that there is a sacred and vast dimension within each of us and, some would add, within all life. Through the ages mystics from all religions and traditions have tried to communicate to the world a sense of the divine presence, at times by relating their personal experiences. They have done this through art, music, dance, meditation, or simply living lives full of love. There are a number of ways. Despite human projections and abstraction, these experiences have been similar enough for one mystic to recognize and accept the experiences of another.

Mystical perceptions touch another-world reality of love, joy, and peace. In the past, and even now, mystics have often withdrawn from the world, for their views and standards have been so strange to people whose view is purely materialistic that antagonism arises. Mystical points of view have not been valued by most people, who consider them unsuitable, inefficient, or worthless. After all, Jesus was crucified. If one has not had encounters of nonmaterial realities, the words of mystics may seem to be nonsense. Attempts to describe mystical experience through intellectual reasoning or from secondhand quotations are simply guesswork. There are those called to the spiritual life who name a genuine turning to God "conversion" or "being born again," but that is not necessarily the same as the mystical experience. Perhaps one difference between these two categories is that generally those with direct experience do not draw absolute conclusions and respect all approaches to religion, while others, in their fervent response, are more likely to condemn approaches different from their own.

Often the mystical experience is likened to falling in love. We idealize romantic love, for it brings us a piercing connection with life that makes us feel truly alive. Yet when we fall in love, we project our ideals on the other, not realizing that our ideals are within ourselves. But through personal love we can come to a greater love. When we are in love, God is close to us because we are in a state of sensitive openness, even though it is focused on one person. Love stories can have a great impact. In most cases the love between two people either lessens or deepens through the stresses of real life. Yet in my experience, I know it is possible, at any moment we choose, to feel love, the love of the Beloved, so deeply as to be moved to tears.

In my life experiences, I have found that everyday life is far more meaningful in all ways, when I follow the attitude implicit in the mystical experience. In any case, I believe that becoming aware of the mystical realms is part of a dynamic process for all humans. The more deeply we encounter the sacred, the more we are sensitive to acting creatively in response to world conditions. Mother Theresa is a good example of someone who served the divine in everyday living.

A Blockage Between Us and the Beloved

One blockage to contacting the Beloved is that, in our loving, we have let our personal desires and perceptions limit us. I was helped out of this limitation by Sheena. She became a midwife for a new birth in many people, symbolized by the birth of the

Christ child in the heart. She had a knack of knowing what would bring on that inner birth. Generally, each of us has something or someone that stands between us and the wisdom of love, something that is given more importance. She saw that I put my marriage and my husband before everything, that I had interpreted my first consciously followed intuition that I was to marry him to mean that the marriage was to be forever. Yet our wedded relationship had become one in which we were more like brother and sister. He used me to escape from involvement with other women, while I, shy and introverted, put him on a pedestal, used him as my mentor, and depended on him for my stability in a country where I had no friends of my own.

After unsuccessfully attempting to bring us closer together, Sheena eventually received an inner message for me suggesting that he would be better off without me. The intimation was that I should consider acting on that premise. I immediately recognized truth in what she said and realized that my love was possessive and selfish. I wanted to have an unpossessive love and, as a seeker, ardently desired to do the right thing, but I did not think I was capable of letting him go. At that time my husband, who was still in British intelligence, had been transferred to Berlin, which, after the Russians closed all roads to the West, was an island in Russian-controlled territory. The Allies instituted an airlift to bring in food and keep the contact. I was not allowed to join him at this critical time. In my willingness to do the right thing, I spent a year genuinely trying to be unselfish. Every day after work I studied papers and books on love, mainly from Sufi teachings, hoping to find clues to help me become unpossessive and unconditional in my love. I would test myself by asking if I was ready for a divorce, for his sake— the ultimate act of unselfishness as far as I was concerned. I found great difficulty in reaching such readiness through the mere reading of papers! But I was determined, and all my energy went wholeheartedly into this aim of gaining a less limited love.

Out of the blue one day, as I was sitting alone in my apartment drinking coffee, I had my first encounter with a most tremendous love. Suddenly I had the awesome experience that I was part of a universal wholeness, that in me was a love so great that my only word for it was God. God was inside and part of me. My world reversed; I was no longer a lonely reject. My touching of divinity at that time changed me so much that friends who saw me the next day told me that I was different, that my voice had changed, and they asked what had happened. I had no answer for them. I was radiant and joyful, and all was well with my world—although of course I did not stay on the mountain-top. That inner experience was the turning point of my life. I was finally capable of dealing with my problem and my personal relationship, going through almost effortlessly with a divorce that would have previously been impossible, though at first I had many moments of self-pity and loneliness.

Not long afterward, whenever I was not concentrating on something, a recurrent thought kept relentlessly intruding, asking me to stop, listen, and write. I resisted. What would I be listening to? Was it safe? What was I getting into? For days and weeks the thought persisted. Finally, in order to get rid of it, I got out my shorthand notebook, hoped I was safe, and, filling myself with memories of my wonderful inner experience, listened within. Uplifting thoughts and feelings came to me, and I chose the words to interpret their meaning. At first I censored the loving thoughts, writing down only what I believed to be true from my Christian and cultural upbringing and my store of wisdom, such as "I am love." Still the original thought persisted, and I continued to record my inspirations, still duly censored. When eventually I shared them with Sheena, she approved of the writings, asked me why I was not doing what I was asked to do, and suggested that I attune three times daily. At the time I certainly needed the discipline and support of a teacher. Otherwise I would never have considered those times of communion important enough to continue. Sheena was the only person from whom I would have accepted the idea of such schooling, for what she said rang true to me. It can help to listen to a personal teacher until we come to trust our own inner promptings. Her support helped me stop censoring and translate the inner meaning as accurately as possible, with a thesaurus as an aid.

Touching Love

My daily explorations into that wholeness were periods that revealed to me a little of the nature of the relationship between God and the human soul. Although the quality of that presence was inexpressible, each day I tried to put into words something of the sensitivities being shared with me. Each time, I was bathed in some aspect of the deepest peace, the purest love, the highest joy, in a condition in which everything was connected—there are no adequate words, so I have to use superlatives. Moreover, each session contained a theme helpful to me: I never knew what it would be and was asked to have no preconceived notions or expectations. Of course, I could receive and translate only according to my understanding, which was continually broadened in the process. The purpose seemed to be to help me apply to my everyday living the pure qualities and perspectives encountered in the presence of God. Each time I entered and was immersed in these personal yet universal dimensions so much greater than my normal awareness, I emerged a more pleasant, freer person—and hoped that my happy state would last more than a few seconds! Over the years, it did become more constant and natural to be aware of a part of myself other than what I considered my faulty personality.

The purity of those dimensions was so great that sometimes I was affected emotionally, but they were not emotional dimensions, nor were they intellectual or logical. They asked me to throw away the critical, analyzing mind and attune to the universal mind. Intellect and logic were perceived from a different perspective in these dimensions. They were areas beyond yet encompassing heart and mind, and beautiful beyond belief. They were beyond *belief*, for they were real. I was asked to live my ordinary life imbued with the quality of love I was experiencing. They uncovered the finest of me, made me realize that my core, everyone's core, is wonderful and can be expressed on every level of our being. It was and is a long process of unfolding, for I had been entrenched in limitation, as many of us are.

At first, at Sheena's suggestion, I always began by asking for cleansing and purifying, because I was afraid of writing nonsense. As another safeguard, I would envision myself surrounded by light, and ask for protection and truth. Then I would choose to imagine myself to be in the inner space in which I had first found God's love. During those times of communion I did not hear or see anything. When necessary, I continued to use a dictionary or thesaurus to translate what I experienced into the most appropriate words I could find. I realized not only that the translation into words brought the sharing down into another dimension, but also that it was helpful to be able to free my mind for the next thoughts while retaining the earlier ones to refer to later. This process tapped into my creativity.

Touching the sacred is not a duty, it is a joy. Looking back, I realize with what incredible wisdom my being was met. What had meaning to me, what was dear to me, was highlighted, emphasized, made strong. My messages were poetic, even whimsical, invoking my sensitivity. I loved them; they expressed my innermost being. God meets us at our vulnerable points and draws out our uniqueness. What was imparted to me was that I was to put love, God, first in my life; this theme was repeated in many different and engaging ways, always delighting me with its touch of beauty. For years I imbibed the love and joy and reassurance of the communion and could always choose to return to it at any time.

In those early days I needed love and guidance. I received it. This transcription was written at a time when God used the metaphor of a stream of love for some weeks.

⌘

Stretch every particle of yourself toward me, and I will fill every particle with myself out of my abundance. Soak yourself in the stream of love inside and out, giving yourself up completely. Relax in it, drown in it, every atom of you, until there is nothing in you not made new and pure.

Then breathe again, like a newly emerged chick, breathing love in instead of air. It is my love that keeps you alive, that sustains you. Know this, breathe it in softly, breathe it out gently.

Let all your thoughts come to love for their life, that they breathe forth my dimensions of love. Let all your acts come to love for their life, that they abound only with love. Let all you see be seen in love, that you see only boundless loveliness.

Walk tentatively in this world of love, letting me guide each step. Stay very young; this is the land of eternal youth and you will lose your way if you grow up. Let every particle of yourself remain in love, and you will never lose your way again. Go onward in the stream of love.

During the meditation I was breathing love in and out, as suggested. But in my ordinary life, though I would try to remember those moments of love, I was just my normal, unloving, personality-centered self. It took years before I would more specifically, and delightedly, follow such instructions. I learned that when I am depressed or feeling cut off, it is not that the flow of inner love has ceased, but that I have severed the connection by my focus on my problems—though knowing it is my own fault doesn't always help!

I needed greater understanding and received it. The following transcription on the patience of God is an example. Remember that it was written more than forty years ago and couched in the terms of my viewpoint then. Now, with a broader perception, I would phrase the ideas very differently, for to me God does not weep, is not limited to masculinity, does not perceive error or good and evil as described here. At the time, however, the message was appropriate.

⌘

Just listen to me in the living stillness, and let me slowly waft my ideas out to you. Gently I will turn a wheel in front of you to present a new face, to unravel another aspect of the ball of love.

Each strand is a living dream, coming to life in my infinite patience, guarded and nurtured in love. The strands are my gifts to you and yet are a part of me, subtly entwining your awareness to my proximity. They move invisibly and inexorably from me and to me.

This is my patience, which nothing can ruffle, which through the aeons drops on, and on, and on, until sometime one small particle of it makes an impression, brings a gift acceptable to a child bound up in the mistakes and misjudgments of the ages. These are the wheels of fate, grinding, grinding, pulverizing, digesting infinitely and ultimately wearing down all the chains that bind my children to error, ceaselessly grinding to make the friction to ignite the spark of love.

Never, never, is there a letup, a resting, a waxing or waning, for then might a child become pledged to the darkness. The mills keep turning, and turning, and turning, with a continuity of purpose that could bring madness to the mind of man. Utter dedication, endless slow motion, the patience of God. Infinitely churning, squeezing the good out of evil to save his children. Tears that never stop dropping, a heart that never stops aching, wearing away the cankers in the hearts of my children. On, and on, and on, the wheels keep turning, the wheels that are made of compassion.

Dry your eyes; this is only one strand in my tapestry of love. Remember my joy, remember my beauty, remember the imp, and give me your love.

I often reread this message, for the words seemed to drift slowly in front of me like falling petals. They were relevant to my need for support, reassurance, and uplift. My needs were met on my level, through the media meaningful to me at the time.

Feeling Love

I needed to be loved, and I was, as the following message attests.

⌘

Come closer, come closer, so softly, on tiptoe. As quietly as a mouse creep up to me. Let me draw you nearer, in slow motion lest we disturb anyone, lest we raise any dust. Move closer to me, invisibly, hearing no evil, seeing no evil, speaking no evil. Only purity can come close to me, and we do not want any ripple of impurity to trip you.

Draw nearer, draw nearer, with the movement of your heart.

Let it expand into me, let it bridge any space between us, until there is just one big flowing heart, so big that it holds up the universe.... Be part of my heart, blood of my blood, my child.

It is my personal disposition to dislike repetition. I am amazed and awed that through the years the Beloved conveyed to me one idea—to love—and conveyed that idea differently each time, using varying and interesting approaches to the theme. I was never bored!

Accepting Oneself with Love

Through the years I continued to start the day with an inner attunement, and through the years the contents deepened, no doubt as I changed with its help and with the experiences presented to me. My needs were always met, and the guidance given helped me grow. Here is an example after about twenty years of "listening."

⌘

When you are in a state of loving, you do not have to try to force contact with me, for I am here. Bitter self-examinations do not bring you to me, and the tension of striving blocks me, but the flow of love, particularly to me, aligns you in harmony. The more directed the flow, the more perfectly your world turns around.

I do not mean that you are not to examine yourself. Search yourself, find the truth of what you are, and in the acceptance of that truth, you are free for love to flow. It is when you do not accept the truth of your faults, when you resist them and so stay emotionally attached and in conflict about yourself, that you remain on the treadmill of the old. Accept the truth, and you are released and relaxed and can become aware of me. Then the love flows. My gigantic reality transcends all else, and all is well. You are reoriented and stabilized, and what comes to you is not right nor wrong but part of you, part of me, in the power of love. Then you can meet and transmute any situation without trying.

I know you do not stay in that state—if you did, you would not need this advice—but when you find yourself out of it, you can choose to turn and come to me again. As you do this, increasingly you will find the love flowing. Everything is on your side: the onward rhythm of evolution, the new energies being expressed, the place you are in, the desire of your soul, and my beckoning love. This is a time of increased opportunity. Go with it, accepting yourself as you are without a quibble and accepting and knowing the reality of what I am in you with joy, thanksgiving, wonder, and love. I make all things new. Love me simply, without strain, and be one with all.

I have looked back in amazement at some of these teachings, for only now, after another twenty years, do I begin to understand them more deeply and differently. For example, the following message is just now becoming real in me:

⌘

As it is right and proper for a child to obey its earthly parents until it comes to its maturity, so it is right and proper for you to obey me, your heavenly Father/Mother, until you come to your spiritual maturity. After that you have all the faculties within you to make your own decisions without turning as a supplicant to me.

This does not mean that you do not do my will. It simply means that you do my will on your own, as the angels do. They do not continually turn to me in consciousness, seeking what is right for them to do; they flow with the energies, and it is impossible for them to do anything but my will. So with you, when you are mature. Because your consciousness is one with the highest, there is no question of returning to the state of separation and having to seek my will. It simply is in you.

You fear that you are not mature enough to be free of your separated self, that subtly it may encroach. As you flow with events and cease thinking in terms of limitation, accepting your maturity, you are living in it, and all is well. Put away childish things; do not cling to them. What if you feel it is a dangerous doctrine for many? You get on with living your own life. You have grown up. Just as your earthly parents trusted you and set you free, I would do no less, knowing that we are bound forever in love and more than that, that we are together always. You are no longer my dutiful child but the Beloved who loves all creation in me, and we both know it and therefore can be one.

Attuning Differently

It was a year or so after receiving this guidance that I knew it was right for me to leave Findhorn and return to my own continent. I decided to stop engaging in the regular morning meditations I had kept up for many years. It was not that I decided to cease attuning; it was that I wanted to be in a state of attunement at all times, not just during a special time in the morning. This is still my goal. What is appropriate for us changes. There definitely seems to be a rhythm in human affairs!

Naturally, all of us experience inner realities differently. The love and intelligence that I call God knows best how to deal with each of us and is always presenting to us the experiences we need for our unfolding. I repeat, the sacred is not confined to helping us through the type of conscious contact that I put into writing. In meditation some people see visions or hear a voice or music, or solve problems. Others have never heard of meditation and know how to meet life in a loving way. They just know intuitively. My own contact has changed since those early days, too. We are all unique, and we are all sustained in different ways. But we draw to ourselves that which is for our deepest good, and we can speed the process through our free will. Certainly my inner contact made me more whole and happier. I know that some people believe that interiorizing separates us from our environment; this was never the case for me, and, in fact, the whole point was to bring into my everyday actions the love I found within. The Beloved would say, "Brush your teeth with me," or "Keep the love flowing."

In my first year at Findhorn and after I had been meditating for ten years, my attention was turned to the natural environment far more deeply. I was asked from within to connect and harmonize with the essence of nature. On attuning to the plant kingdom, I found that each species had an intelligent soul in charge of it. Here, too, was the love of God. The souls of the kingdoms of nature, whether of mineral, plant, or animal, I called angels or devas. They had one factor in common: they were continuously God-conscious. Their praise and awareness helped me become more aware of the sacred in my life. They were continuously loving, with a love broad and inclusive enough to contain everything equally. At first that equality of loving struck me as cold and detached, for I had been expecting a love specifically directed to me, as human love is. I did not recognize its depth. Angelic love is impersonal. God's love is directed to everything and is also in each one of us specifically; it is both impersonal and personal. I explored cooperation with nature and the results as they are expressed in a garden and community in *To Hear the Angels Sing*.

Belief or faith in a greater realm or connectedness within us can help us consider our everyday routine as meaningful and relevant. Our belief forms our own level of consciousness before we know. Such belief is natural and has been encouraged in all cultures. Walking purposelessly in a chaotic universe, not fitting into any scheme and having no belief or connectedness, as our present culture describes reality, is paralyzing. I think this is the first time in history that humans have invented such a superficial interpretation of life. There just isn't much point to life when nothing matters or when what matters is merely getting ahead of the other person, amassing possessions or money. That divine discontent within us urges us to find something beyond our present situation. According to the psychotherapist Stanislav Grof, there is ample evidence that the transcendental impulse is the most vital and powerful force in human beings. R. J. Stewart, author of many books on the Celts, writes that compassion is the most potent power that can be filtered through to the human state in the outer world, and that its operation cuts across all other cycles of power. That "something" we are urged to seek is eventually unveiled as the wholeness called God. We need to know the truth—that we are part of a greater-than-normal consciousness, that our identity is vast. We need to sense wonder in life. Both group and individual love can lead us to that vastness.

Grounding Love

Wonderful, deep, loving, and complete as my continuing inner attunements were, they were just a beginning, for what use are the greatest inspirations unless they are realized in ordinary living? Admittedly, those periods of meditation changed me, imbuing me with a love that gradually seeped into my personality and always suggesting that I practice love in my everyday life. I had, and still have, much to transform. As always, life brought me the situations that opened for me opportunities for choice and change.

There are those who have an inner knowing of what is and what is not true for them, without an actual vivid experience. All of us have our own intimations of immortality in some way, though our culture doesn't recognize or teach us how to interpret such hints. This knowing is not just faith; it is deeper than faith or belief. It is not just to the mystics that we look for expressions of connections to the wholeness of life, but to something within ourselves. We are born with inner knowing, and we reach a point where outer authority is not as relevant as inner authority. Even then, we tread a razor's edge between doubt and knowledge. People have told me how lucky I am to have clear inner guidance about what to do. It always seemed a grace, but it was not just poured in, and I had to really focus on it. Guidance has been like a very still small understanding toward which I have had to stretch to hear, leading me to an ever greater sensitivity. Often I have doubted it.

Many people today believe that the best way to focus on wholeness is to deal with our personality difficulties and limitations before we begin to tread the spiritual path. It is assumed that one cannot encounter a pure spiritual level until one has cleared one's character at the psychological level. This is certainly a logical perception, but life is not always logical. It is by commitment or by a mysterious grace that we open to spirit. It has not been my experience that sorting out personality problems first is necessary, and since we are human, this will never be entirely possible. By focusing on our difficulties, whether mental, emotional, or physical, we often circle around with them like rats on a wheel. I left personal conceptions behind and touched the heights, which moved me so powerfully that all of my being, including the personality, was affected and changed for the better. My mind and emotions were naturally engaged as I linked up in consciousness to a dimension beyond what was normal to me. My entire being was, and is, gradually changed in the presence of the Beloved, and I chose day-to-day access to it. Sheena's teaching and example helped me align with my greater self, and her discipline helped weed out much of my "ego," so that I was able to be a reasonably clear mirror for truth.

I believe that one of the goals of people in the present age is not to follow a perfected guru, as in the past in the East. Our Western path is that of the individual, and even the supposedly least enlightened individual is part of God and can experience divinity and follow his or her unique destiny. Among our Western models are people who touch the heights, yet still have many faults and are not ashamed to admit their mistakes. The spiritual teacher and student Ram Dass is a good example. We three founders of Findhorn, Eileen and Peter Caddy and I, were obviously very ordinary, imperfect people. We have been taken as models, and our ordinariness is our strength: if we can touch something divine—and we did—then anyone can. The point is that anyone can. We are part of the sacred all the time unconsciously, or we could not draw breath or have a heartbeat or experience emotions and thoughts. To be aware of what we are, of our divinity, and to live it on Earth is our loving destiny.

Divinity in All Life?

From years of turning to that greater part of me, I can only affirm that we live in a universe in which God is the ultimate reality and mystery. It took me a long time to accept divinity in all life. There are so many aspects of humanity that seem to harbor no God or good, places where there is starvation, injustice, cruelty, violence. Some think that if a God existed, he or she or it would not permit such evil. To gain any sort of understanding of these seemingly unfair situations, my perspectives had to be broadened to admit that we humans have free will in creating and dealing with these conditions. When I am cruel or violent, it is because I have lost the connection with my center of lovingness. In my life I realized that I have the freedom to choose love and bring it into every aspect of my life. The love that gives us free choice is greater than the love that expects only obedience. I found that it is our reactions that make or mar situations and that life is eternal and not confined to just one opportunity. I discovered that adversity is often a better teacher than affluence, that resistance and the suffering that results from it are spurs to make us grow. We cannot continue to use others or God as our scapegoat. I found that in my darkest times I learned and transformed most. Difficulties were opportunities, and when I failed, I could say, "Well, I've blown it again, but I can choose differently next time." And though I live alone, I am not alone, for I am part of a loving whole.

We can refute a divine presence, but we cannot refute the power through which we are conscious. In scientific terms, all that we are conscious of is derived, received, or abstracted from Light/Energy/Living Matter. We flounder for words when referring to God and to the angelic realm, both of which are beyond reach of our ordinary senses. All our words are tied to the sensory world. In trying to explain the sacred, we lose contact. Yet we already have basic awareness, and we can practice mindfulness.

Putting God first is not just following guidance or commandments, though this is an invaluable stage. Instead, putting God first means that one enters into a closer relationship with the love within. One can choose to do this rather than just being obedient. A way to clarify or free our emotional selves is by accessing our spiritual selves. Meditation is a way to nurture what is already within us. Planted in us is a profound longing that transcends romantic and parental love; this divine discontent is the basis of evolutionary striving. If we love someone, we want to be with him or her, to laugh together; in the same way, we can choose to be with God and find love and joy. Intuition and inspiration are means by which our connection with the divine is made conscious. Whether we work for this connection or it just happens, it is always a gift. It happens at odd times and for odd purposes. Most geniuses and inventors tell stories of tapping into a higher "something."

Consciousness of the Beloved

In my experience, touching the sacred in meditation takes us into the realm of essence above the senses. Guided imagery can bring us into a peaceful state, which aids us to go deeper. It suits me best to go directly into the realm of essence. Another method is to seek an inner divine child, playful and magical, or an inner wise old man to guide us; contacting these and other aspects of our inner world are ways of gaining access to the God within. God uses whatever means there are for helping a human soul toward freedom and oneness, and all techniques can help and are therefore of God.

In no way can I do justice to the glory and joy of that divine presence. We have such a pitiful notion of God, of love. We have so few words or concepts to express love. We do not understand that love "passeth all understanding." We do not see how love can be the ultimate truth and can have intelligence, for what we know as human love does not seem intelligent. We have a sentimentally sweet idea of love—and indeed, when it is restricted to the emotions, it is somewhat powerless. But the love that imagined the universe as something to love has no restrictions, except in our human minds. Love, as spoken of in I Corinthians, chapter 13 (which, besides being

Sheena's favorite biblical passage, was also the one that my university sorority used as its Bible quotation), means believing all things, hoping all things, enduring all things. That is true, but it also creates all things, knows all things. It is a state of being, the most satisfying state there is. It comes from within. We underestimate it and always will, for there is a mystery here and always will be.

We even say that God is not powerful. Since divine power manifests in our affairs according to our ability to love, which is generally small, we find little evidence of that power. It is there; we just don't see it when we grant power to the material level. It is the individuals who are anchored in God who have the power to stand on their own and not be submerged in the mass.

My desire to write, however inadequately, of the numinousness that I call God comes from the impact God's presence had on my consciousness. There is nothing I would like more than to aid others in opening to that tremendous love, as I myself was aided. Sometimes I think I am a fanatic in my desire to emphasize the purity of God! Writing of the process of turning inward and of touching that presence is not easy. Spiritual techniques or practices in all religions are aimed at helping people have an experience of God. In our present world of instant gratification, there may be disappointment in following a technique that seems to bring no results. One reason for the widespread use of drugs is that they at least give an instant awareness of another level of being, though not necessarily a helpful one. Dedication and commitment to the spiritual life bring their own rewards, such as a feeling of "rightness," and may or may not lead to a mystical experience. Actual knowing, coming from intuition or inner guidance, imparts tremendous strength; one feels that one can do or face anything, that everything is grist for the mill; we find synchronicity a companion. I have had experiences in my life when I knew I had to do something, and with that knowing, nothing could stop me. Since the divine is our core, eventually we become aware of that relationship through the practice of life.

Gaining Access to the Beloved in Action

The astounding love of the Beloved is the core of each one of us, no matter how we denigrate ourselves. Only from that core of ourselves can we fulfill our function in and for the world. That divine area in us is always unfolding. It never gives up. It is important for us to realize that we are surrounded on all sides by God, by love, and that where we are is where we are meant to be.

All our senses, visible and invisible, are our God-given faculties for full awareness in action. When we are in a loving state, the love shines through all our actions and influences everything around us. And everything around us has an answer to our questions, because we are all part of the same life. In some workshops I have given, participants spent a day alone in nature, and it was marvelous to hear their stories of how an insect, a bird, a twig gave the answers they were seeking. Even though in our culture sacredness stands apart from everyday living, sacredness really is in us and all about us when we adjust our view. In every act we deal with the sacred.

The Beloved and Change

Change in our way of seeing, change in our attitude, comes about as we flow with the experiences life offers us, for behind even the most troublesome circumstances are harmony and purpose. We become painfully aware that all aspects of the planet, or of our body, are interconnected when our mismanagement of one part affects another. We can help bring to light the hidden harmony when we choose to do the best we can in any circumstance. We can choose to act from our divine center, for the grace and mystery of God and the universe are with us, and all creation is headed toward fulfillment. I wouldn't be surprised if just as we are now finally realizing that we are part of the environment, part of the living planet, we soon come to know we are part of God. We are partners in life.

I think of Christ as the aspect of God in all life actively connecting us to the divine, empowering us to meet daily life with love as our ally. The birth of love, of Christ, in us, which is our first awareness of God within, is a cosmic event, an event that is continually arising in us. The God in each of us, in its longing to surface, attracts to us again and again exactly the situations we need to help us develop. We are ever expanding, always becoming, in a manner akin to the growth of a baby, and yet at the same time we are complete.

Every great teacher has propounded a path to our future, and at this time of desperate need for our planet, these paths are becoming ever clearer. There will always remain a mystery to awaken awe and lead us on. We are being called to rouse ourselves, to awaken the sensitivity to respond to the very structure of reality, which will align us with the unfolding of the Earth's process. The uncovering of the soul is the discovery of God, revealing our wholeness, our intelligence, all life's creative core.

Summary

The key is love, the action is service, and the joy is knowing the grandeur that is God in us and in everything. As we love, we are connecting with our core, and at some point we become aware of that inner love. We might spend happy hours (or unhappy hours if we don't feel connected) in meditating and experiencing love within. But we are here to live on the planet, not merely to spend our time contemplating a single level of life. We are here to connect with love and bring it to Earth wisely, and the way to do that is by serving creation on Earth with body, mind, and soul. Joy follows, for serving is a deeply intrinsic characteristic within us as human beings. When we serve, we are loving, wise, light-filled, peaceful, and creative. We are expressing God the Beloved.

Exercise:

The exercises I am suggesting are practices that have helped me through the years. Because each person is unique, one's practices are also unique. I can only share what has been important to me. If you are worried, as I used to be, that you might contact only your own desires or mistaken notions, or even an evil entity, you can surround yourself with light; pray for cleansing and purifying, and call upon whatever helps you to feel safe and protected. You can ask for the highest good for all concerned.

We have all had peak experiences that have taken us out of our everyday awareness. Such an expansion is sparked by different experiences for each of us, whether it be the beauty of a sunset or some other aspect of nature, or a smile, or music. We can remember that moment and relive it, using our memory and imagination to create a similar inner state. That state is the highest one we know, our known experience of God.

Positively choose to be in the feeling of the inner space of that revived memory. Immerse yourself in it; let its love and joy flood your being, absorb its qualities. Then become responsive, receptive, still focused on the highest. Listen sensitively, or ask a question. Be open to what the universe is communicating to you, or simply absorb the beauty of it, the feel of it. Communication from that realm comes in various forms, so do not let expectations close any doors. Remain open and free.

If you do receive a message, trust it and act on it. When something is conveyed from that state, know that it comes from the highest level of being and that action stemming from it is appropriate. If you don't receive any specific communication, accept it without anxiety. Resonating with the vibrations of the inner space, absorbing its purity, may be all that is needed,

This exercise is the start for connecting not only with the sacred within but also with any part of creation, for all creation holds the essence of God. Connections on personality levels are open to all the limitations of our materialistic viewpoints and backgrounds; connections to the inner presence cover greater and wiser realms.

CHAPTER TWO

POLARITIES AND CHOICES

Good and Evil

If the core of the universe is love, where does evil come in? Did God create evil? Are good and evil opposite, battling dualities, as I was taught, or are they harmonious intertwined complementaries as diagrammed by the Chinese yin/yang symbol? Such questions have long puzzled me, and I am always grappling with them. I have realized in my thought and experience that these opposites are interlocked, for how could we be aware of light without the comparison of darkness or sound without quietude? The pairs of opposites are inseparable, one impossible without the other.

In our dynamic universe, we describe the alignment of physical properties through systems of polarities, positive and negative. According to the benefit we derive or the value we put on polarities, we usually judge them as good or bad. There are many different perceptions of evil, but, in general, something we regard as hurtful to us is called evil. It might be a force we consider malevolent, like an earthquake, or a fear or a demonic being. Evil can be considered merely the complement or shadow of good, or the illusion of independent existence, separateness from God. Some consider that because life is movement, evil is the curtailment of liberty, as in living in authoritarian states or groups. Evil is also thought to derive from misplaced timing or from a craving for power. It is also said to be the spirit that cannot abide change unless it controls change; this aspect of evil arises when an evolving consciousness becomes fixated on something and makes it permanent. A definition I like is that evil is stuck energy, something many of us experience when our neck pains us when we have long remained in one position, but which applies on most levels. Buddhists believe that suffering, which we consider evil, stems from our own cravings. The Hopis understand suffering as the work of an evil community. Christians blame Satan. Some people consider evil to be merely the law of contraction, the bringing down of spiritual energies into physical matter, which is a process necessary to creation. Many of our negative values come from faulty or limited human judgments that result in "wrong" actions. We analyze evil and come to many differing definitions, and we call them negative. On the whole, we attribute bad qualities to the word "negative." But however many ideas we may entertain, mostly we still value light above dark.

Our cultures, our societies, have neatly codified various aspects of life into what is good and what is bad. We always think in terms of opposites, though we normally consider God to be wholly good. We have made rules, laws, taboos. We have needed a code of behavior for the smooth flow of social interaction, and we sustain the collective values of our race by allowing and accepting them. Although our lists of what is proscribed and what is sanctioned, the "bads" and "goods," generally agree all over the world, there are still great differences in cultures; in Polynesia, obesity is a positive attribute, in North America it is not accepted. Burping is encouraged in one place, discouraged in another. We in the West live in an either/

or society, and our fashions, what we like and dislike, change rapidly. Today authority is often considered a curtailment of our right to freely express ourselves, but I believe many personal commandments and laws are applicable and helpful, until the time comes when our judgment and wisdom reach a certain maturity. An example of a personal code conflicting with a societal code might be when a mother steals bread to save the life of her starving child.

Our societal rules begin exerting an influence on us the moment we are born. It is bad for a baby to cry and good for a baby to be quiet. When a dog obeys a command, it is called "good dog." When the dog doesn't obey, it is a "bad dog." From our first breath we live in an atmosphere of such wrongs and rights, until our world takes shape in the context of good and evil.

We do not identify ourselves completely with either good or evil, though we generally would like to be good. We haven't come to recognize the value in darkness, in negativity, or in the inertia that in a quiescent period of germination serves growth. We don't see that if we lived in the light all the time, it would kill us. For me, it was always out of a time of seeming darkness and aloneness that new development arose. I remember discovering in my astrological chart a certain extremely dark and difficult period in my life, which I found was the time when I was tackling my divorce and trying to be unselfish. It was at that point that the Beloved came through to me and changed my life into one of meaning and purpose through the growth of love. It is often through crisis that awareness dawns on an unaware person, restoring balance. Throughout history, both for individuals and countries, it is after a time of trouble, a period of chaos, that there has been a new emergence. We make our distinctions between good and bad, and the point of separation, the boundary, is a wavering line drawn according to our current perspective. We concentrate on one side of the line, whether we call it a separating or a meeting point. We unceasingly strive for the good, the pleasure, and run from the bad. However much we adhere to the notion that the pairs of opposites are part of each other, on the whole we still choose what we consider the good. We sustain our cultural upbringing— and, of course, all my ruminations are colored by my Western point of view.

Yet, as we recognize in working with electricity, the positive and the negative are simply two poles, neither good nor bad. The positive force is what activates or stimulates the negative substance, for expression at any level needs material to shape. There is polarity throughout life: night and day, winter and summer, destruction and creation. For example, sad as it made me at the time, I found that the destruction of the beautiful flowering gorse was necessary before a vegetable or flower garden could grow where I was living in Scotland. Life could not proceed without destruction, yet we consider most forms of destruction to be bad, negative.

Eastern and Western Views

In Zoroastrianism, Judaism, and Christianity, life is a conflict of the forces of light and those of darkness. The dogmas of the Christian church are based on the intellectual underpinnings of Greek philosophy, following Aristotle's polarizing logic that all action is based on choice. This perspective led to extreme dualism and spawned the Christian mythology of Satan and Hell, and a doctrine of eternal, implacable strife. In the Egyptian pantheon, Osiris and Set are twin brothers, yet conflict begins between them. In other traditions, evil is defined relative to where one stands, and pain is part of the very existence of a world; the process of life hurts even though it is wonderful. In Hindu thought there is no sin, only ignorance. Life is a cosmic dance, *lila*, in which those with true integrity do not choose, but play the game, dealing in comprehension with what comes their way. The devils, or asuras, of Hinduism and Buddhism are simply dark forces of the divine, which is in itself beyond good and evil. In Taoism, the yin and yang principles do not conflict with but rather complement each other; positive and negative are relative, conditional, with no intrinsic distinction between them. In mythological stories black generally represents what cannot be consciously known, the nocturnal and earthly, while white stands for daylight and clarity but can be either a negative or a positive attribute. But we in the West are brought up to believe that light is good, or positive, and dark is bad, or negative.

The discoveries and explorations of the Swiss philosopher Carl Gustav Jung about those aspects of our human makeup that he called the collective unconscious and the shadow have tremendously influenced our Western views of good and evil. In large measure thanks to his work, and a general acceptance of his theories as scientific, perspectives have been changing from blaming others for our ills to acknowledging that we project our own problems outside ourselves. If we are the author of our difficulties, are we bad? Do we create evil? We feel we are not really evil, though we may have our moments.

Choices and Judgments

At first, even in my meditations the idea of a good and bad duality in me was emphasized. I had thought of myself only as a very limited and awkward personality, which I called my "lower" self, while in meditation I was aware of a wonderful, loving, knowing self. I was, as we all are, paradoxically both human and divine. Having always been focused on the outer world, I had to experience a deep immersion in my greater inner self to admit to its presence. At the time, I considered my divine self good, but I would get fed up with and condemn my erring personality. I hadn't learned to appreciate my humanness. This dichotomy was accentuated in my early Findhorn days, for when some idea or project was being discussed and I offered an opinion, Peter Caddy would say, "I don't want to know what you think; I want to know what God thinks." In his way he was seeking the best guidance for Findhorn, but personally I would feel crushed and inadequate. I was forced to turn within and experience my more comprehensive self. At the time, I resented my situation; now I am grateful. I needed that type of discipline to point me beyond my surface focus. Not until I got fed up with my resentment and chose to see what I considered the good in Peter instead of what I considered the bad, did my resentment vanish, whereupon Peter treated me differently as well.

I kept thinking that surely in terms of the essentials of life there are definite acts of good and evil. Murder is bad; being helpful is good. That murder is considered good in wartime did not enter my thoughts then! Surely the good is better than the bad? Surely they can't be utterly equal? Many things confirmed my belief that the good in some way outweighs the bad.

Through the years the boundary line that I drew between good and evil has blurred. Although like others I judged Hitler as evil, a friend of mine saw a different side of him. In the 1930s she was introduced to him at a party in Munich and, because of her dislike of Nazi behavior, she endangered herself and her date, an S.S. officer, by putting her hands behind her back and refusing to shake hands. To her great surprise, she said, she saw a "Christ light" in Hitler's eyes. Also, the only person outside the family that their dog ever approached was Hitler; several times in restaurants the dog went over to him. I heard a story that in those years Alice Bailey, author of many books presenting the teachings of a Tibetan master I respected, had gone to Hitler to warn him that he had a great capacity to create either good or evil; he was at a crossroads and needed to take special care how he chose. What Hitler chose may have been, to him, what was good or right at the time. Because our failures burn into our egos, we learn more from them than from our successes. We need to ask ourselves, Did he learn, did his nation learn, did the world learn anything from events stemming from all the choices leading to World War II? Do we have to learn the hard way, through suffering, as the Buddhists teach, with our problems being the raw material of our redemption?

I know, because I have experienced it, that a loving God is the core of my being. How could love create evil? Symbolically, in Paradise was placed the tree of the knowledge of good and evil, which God commanded man not to eat from, "for in the day that thou eatest thereof thou shalt surely die." According to the Jewish chroniclers, then, God knew about good and evil. And the subtle serpent said to Eve that she would not die if she ate of that tree but that her eyes would be opened, and she would be as God, knowing good and evil. Eve ate and Adam ate, and God saw that man had become as "one of us," knowing good and evil. "Now, lest he put forth his hand, and take also of the tree of life, and eat, and live forever," God drove man from Eden. Among the symbology of those words, what stands out for me is that the human being who knows good and evil, must not, or cannot, live forever. Knowing of, or depending on, good and evil is a temporary state. Innocent humankind lives in Paradise, until driven out, and humankind that has gone beyond the judgment of good and evil lives in

Paradise, or lives forever. Human beings can be liberated and live beyond judgment, as the angels do.

A pivotal experience in my progress was when I communicated with the angels of qualities and found them to be beyond polarity, encompassing the full spectrum of the opposites. The Angel of Joy and the Angel of Sorrow were one angel, one seed energy. At the time, I merely registered and accepted this as the way things are. I simply understood that our human organization of judgments does not apply in the angelic realm. Not until later did the relevance of this dawn on me. Primary essence contains the seed of all substance before it is manifested, before it splits into polarity. I could not reach these beautiful energies when I was living in a world of judgmental "goods" and "bads"; the angels did not exist at these levels. Gradually I began to see that I could conduct my everyday life better by choosing angelic energies without constantly making judgments.

Need for Conflict

Without polarities or gradations of them, there can be no choice. Conflict gives us choices. Through the tension between opposites we realize imbalance, which produces an opportunity to choose to accept the tension and gives love a chance to surface. If everything were single and whole, there would be only one path, and we would be automatons—as we were before being expelled from Eden. We did not know there was one way, or any way. We just followed our noses, so to speak. Most of us are still slaves to our culture and behave automatically, according to our upbringing. In some old cultures, precepts and behavior patterns are so deeply ingrained that choice does not exist, and one always knows what response one will get to a question or an action. The people of these cultures do not realize their lack of choice, for they naturally respond the way their tribe or culture has always responded. For example, orthodox Jews don't choose not to eat pork, nor do fundamentalist Christians question the literal meaning of the Bible. Without choice, without judgment, in perfect conditions, there would be nothing to learn, nothing to create, nothing to do. Perhaps the world exists to give us the choices from which we learn to love.

Looking at Good and Evil from a New Perspective

The idea of good and evil is something to confront, though we each confront it from where we stand. It plays a major role in our lives, influencing our morals, our ethics, our spirituality, our balance, and our behavior, helping us understand our fears and our disconnection from God. It is an essential element in affecting our choices. I now believe that a deeper understanding of how we judge these opposites, deciding what is positive or negative in our actions, is a very necessary step in our development. In the Bible story of the development of humankind, in Paradise we are at one with the universe, without self-awareness; that is, we don't know what we are or even that we are. We are as unconscious as we believe a leaf to be. Knowledge of the opposites, attributing value to them, is a primary step in human development, the start of self-awareness. Through the development of the mind, the instrument of awareness, comparison, and thus the ability to choose, we begin to know we are separate from others. We begin to identify ourselves. Through us the sacred is then expressed consciously in life, God living in knowing as well as through sense experience. God's driving of Adam and Eve from Eden, like a mother bird ejecting her young from the nest so that they learn to fly, was the first step for humanity in learning to live in consciousness, to choose between what is right and wrong, good and evil, leading eventually to responsibility, maturity, and love/wisdom.

My experience was and is of a God of love, and since love can embrace everything and is the source of everything, I don't believe in a God of evil, a Satan. Even the angels with whom I am in touch, who are lesser than God, can't, or won't, take action against anyone or anything. I don't believe in fallen angels; humankind just found another scapegoat when we blamed Lucifer, the bringer of light, for our own projections of evil. As for our personal capacities for "evil," I believe that if we continue disharmonious behavior or harm any part of the whole, we draw to ourselves balancing energies—which are usually so unpleasant and so painful that we have no alternative but to change and discover a new way. To me the spark of the divine in us, working through our personalities, draws the appropriate conditions to us so that we learn, though we usually call those conditions difficult or even evil.

I found new light on the situation one day. I was searching for assistance to clarify my directions, and turned to Krishnamurti, an enlightened Indian teacher, in his book *Freedom from the Known*. I had read and listened to his words through the years, but this time I actually followed his advice. He said that if we were to look at our faults and failings, at the things we don't like in ourselves, at our sufferings, without judgment, without condemnation, without any movement of thought, without any comfort, just completely holding them and accepting them, then a strange psychological transformation would happen. I did this, with my many faults in mind, and a miraculous transformation did indeed take place: I found myself in the incredible presence of the Beloved. Previously I had always to "rise above" my negativities to reach God. Now I was offering up the negative totally to the whole, being completely receptive, and receiving a positive response, perhaps similar to the way lightning responds to the Earth's negative forces. Since then I have repeated this exercise—for there seems to be no end to what I don't like in myself—and often there is a wonderful liberation, a sense of towering freedom and love. It is very easy for me to be self-critical, to condemn myself for even such a small thing as not phoning my friend Julie to give her birthday greetings when I was reminded of that event a day late. When memory of my omission continued to bother me, I sat down and mentally went over the situation without judgment until it boiled down to "I didn't phone Julie, I didn't phone Julie," as a mere fact, free of emotions and criticism. Somehow I experienced love pouring in. Love swamped me and took over, and I was released, free, loving, no longer feeling the burden of guilt.

This process should not be confused with reprogramming, that is, replacing negative emotions with positive ones, or with using affirmations, procedures that had been helpful to me early on but can lead to denial. We resolve conflict by acceptance. If we deny something, we create opposition, and fighting negativity only gives it more energy. Nonjudgmental perception allows us to experience directly the flow of love and understanding.

The importance of not judging became more significant after this experience of accepting rather than fighting negativity. I was helped on the subject of judgment and guilt by the teachings of Vitvan, an American who brought together Eastern thought from his Shakti Yoga training and Western science from his study of Einstein and semantics. According to him, as we follow the inner call to be ourselves, in developing the ego sense we have to fight against the instinctive, elemental influences of our long past and against the intrusion of the environment. There are many little battles, and every time we fail, we feel guilty. If the guilt sense accumulates and becomes stronger than the ego sense, a reversal in the polarity of our psychic natures is effected, and we accentuate the negative. We become too introverted and hypersensitive, which reflects on the personality as emotional and functional disturbances and organic disorder. Guilt feelings which develop out of failures in the battle engender a fear complex. The most deeply rooted fear is the fear of being cut off from the whole, but we mentally identify it with something else, like fear of being alone. There is no blame in this attitude. It is the natural order, and at this stage one has to fight the guilt and fear. Vitvan estimated that he had failed ten thousand times to one success and suggested we never give up. It certainly made me feel empowered to hear that this master had experienced so many failures! The concept of fighting guilt and fear is valid up to the point where we accept our negativities, which is the point many people have reached in this therapeutic age. At this phase, as Vitvan said, we don't fight; we can accept and change the pattern.

Importance of Choice

To me, choice is vital; it is the method or process by which we realize more of our human and divine nature. It is through choice that we learn. When we choose to put our fingers in a fire and get them burned, we learn about the effects of fire on flesh. I began to learn to focus not on value judgment, but on choice. When we choose spicy dishes, we learn by experience what degree of spiciness suits our palate. When we choose to hurt somebody, we discover how we and others feel about it. At one time we may revel in hating someone. At another time, when we learn to follow our intuitions or guidance and not our reactions to outer circumstances, we learn that we swim in a powerful tide with the forces working in our favor. When we

choose to act against inner feelings, we not only get into difficulties but we generally also feel guilty. I can remember literally
running away from a situation I found myself in as a mother's
helper in a small Scottish city. I felt that the particular task was
mine to face, but didn't want to. There was no means of trans-
port, and hitchhiking had not worked. There was nowhere to
sleep (I tried benches in a railway station and was asked to
move) and nowhere to go, and I had no money. Everything was
against me. I learned how benign our intuition is and how
problems arise from ignoring it.

For me, choice is the essential catalyst for our individual
growth in the West. It is the symbol of our humanity, Hamlet's
ultimate dilemma ("To be or not to be"). It is through choice
that we learn wisdom, that we alter our state of consciousness,
that we know what makes us happy or comfortable or in tune
with the universe. Paradise forced on us might be hell, unless
we choose it as well. When we are small children the experience
of choosing identifies our differences and uniqueness. Through
our choices we learn of ourselves and the world; through our
choices we move to more lessons and experiences. We do have
patterns imposed on us by our culture, the codes necessary for
social life, and by our past, but within those patterns there is
still choice. Choice is forever given to us from within: choice as
to what level of ourselves we wish to function on, choice as to
how clearly we can express our true feeling, the divinity within
us. This decision-making takes practice.

If we are able to keep on choosing, our decisions and their
results will eventually bring us to a realization of "atonement"
with our divine selves, for nothing else can satisfy us. First we
may believe that material possessions, riches, another person,
the moon, will be what we want, and we will vacillate from
one unsatisfying alternative to another, trying to find personal

gratification. Then we may try again. Some people don't need to try hard for results; the plodder has to, and so learns more deeply. Eventually we will find greater fulfillment on the more subtle levels of love, of service, of ideals. Then our choice and greater joy is to do what is "right," the highest that we know. We will in our way listen inwardly to find out what the will of the whole is for us, and we will strive to follow that guidance. Eventually there is but one choice. We attune ourselves to God within us until gradually we don't need to be obedient to it, because we are at one with it. Then our choices are infinitely loving and caring, not only for us but for all concerned in the given situations.

The ability to choose has been, and still is, absolutely vital in the development of Western culture. No matter how often our decisions have been "wrong," limited, biased, selfish, too individualistic, they have been our learning process. For generations, as times changed, pendulums of behavior have swung back and forth. For instance, we think that parents of the Victorian age were too controlling of their young people, and the pendulum has swung to the other direction, to more permissiveness with children. We are still exploring that fine line between "too much" and "too little" discipline, and by our choices we learn. The fashion world gives us choices that also change—short skirts, long skirts, no skirts. Now we are being forced by nature itself to choose to balance our planetary excesses, learning from the planet itself that we must make decisions that encompass more than ourselves if we wish to continue living here. I don't think we Westerners appreciate the power of choice that we have, how precious it is, and how little choice some societies have. Recently a friend of mine told me that she had offered a young man from a Third World country the gift of one of two belts. He had stood in front of her paralyzed, helpless, and very troubled, for he had never had to choose before and didn't know how to do it. Such a situation is unbelievable to us.

Function of the Concept of Good and Bad Choice

But why do I continue, in spite of my rational mind and my spiritual understanding, to elevate "good" behavior above "bad" behavior? Are my cultural background patterns simply so strongly entrenched that I won't or can't change? Fear of change has been defined as the root of evil. One reason I have been loath to give up the concept of good and bad, quite apart from my training, is that it has become habitual in daily use. I can't make a decision without evaluating the situation, even at simple levels: Is going to restaurant A better than going to restaurant B? Though going to restaurant B may not be evil, it is through such choices that we whittle our way to our changing standards. We need the choices to give us meaning in life. Good and evil concepts have been important enough for most religious teachers and saints in the past to stress them, codify them, or just take them so for granted that it is not necessary to mention them. Unless I am intuitive, I make mental or emotional comparisons of what is best for me when I make my decisions.

I keep learning about choices and the stresses in my life. When I stopped resenting the way Peter Caddy treated me and chose to see the good in him, I began to see the value of nonjudgment. More circumstances arose. I have always been driven wild by the thought of missing an airplane flight and upsetting the schedules of friends meeting me and of appointments at the other end of a trip. I was once delayed at U.S. Immigration, where I was rudely questioned at length about certain things, to which I gave uneven answers. I was in fact breaking a law that seemed stupid to me. I kept repeating, "I'll miss my plane!" I had to wait more than half an hour to undergo another interview with the authorities. By then I was beside myself with anxiety, pacing up and down like a caged lion, one part of me even enjoying the adrenaline rush and my annoyance. After the second interrogation I was eventually set free, five minutes after my plane was due to leave. I rushed to the departure point and tore across the floor in such an agitated state that I twisted my ankle and couldn't walk. I managed to hop to the desk and discovered that the plane had been delayed. Talk about lack of trust! I needed a wheelchair there and again when changing planes at Chicago and at my destination, but gradually I walked again. I came to realize, of course, that the stress of my expectations and judgments were the real cause of the physical ailment, though that realization didn't make me feel better!

Shortly after this incident, another opportunity to learn confronted me. On leaving Bangkok at the end of a three-month trip, I found at the airport that my ticket had been canceled and there was no seat for me on the plane. There I was, alone in a foreign country without money, with no place to stay, no one to turn to, no knowledge of the language. I was put on a waiting list. This time I determined not to panic. I chose to attune and kept trying to attune. It was touch and go, but somehow I made it and got a seat on the plane, even though I was not feeling any peace.

A third opportunity arose later in the year. My plane was late in arriving in New York from South America. I always feel like a complete country bumpkin in New York. New Yorkers seem so quick, so all-knowing, so unhelpful that when I ask a question all I receive is a pitying look. There I was, having to find my way to another terminal, with heavy luggage and insufficient time. Fortunately I remembered to get centered and attuned, and chose forthwith to radiate love. To my amazement, everyone, including erstwhile unaccommodating porters, went out of their way to help me, coming to me and asking if I needed them. I did, and was escorted to my plane in record time and in a state of joy. I couldn't believe that all those people could be so different—but, of course, I was the one who was different.

For a time after this experience the power of love worked instantaneous magic in many situations. A problem would arise, and when I chose to accept it and love everything about it, without judgment or expectation, suddenly the phone would ring with my answer, or the solution would appear in some other way. Miracles were working. I was experiencing that the power of love is the strongest force in the universe. And the next time I had trouble getting to a plane on time, instead of panicking, I chose to send love to the lost driver. Although I missed my plane, I could accept the situation. We do learn.

Individual Choice

It is in our individual choices, not society's choices, that we can come closer to our real selves. Society's codes may have told us that it is better to serve than to be served, but when we choose to serve of our own free will, and feel a glow and free-dom in the doing, we truly appreciate and internalize the worth of service. We feel good about it. We like the feeling and are more likely to be of service another time. Even though modern psychology explores the value of service, the emphasis on doing what we want to do and not acting out of old pat-terns or duty often gives the impression that we ought not serve others. Yet we have within us that which likes to be of service and is open to others and to the environment. This feeling has nothing to do with righteousness or duty or with obeying the letter of the law, which are ego responses. Our inner selves are always standing on tiptoe, ready to surface in our consciousness, and we can trust their nudges absolutely. We can always choose to turn to those "higher" energies. Our limitations are a burden until we commit ourselves to the inner, as when my desire to serve my husband drove me to choose to love him more than myself and led me to the Beloved.

If we make a choice to act on the advice of others, however holy or wise or attuned that other may be, we do not engage our freedom of choice, and we do not learn. Others can then be blamed or praised for the results of our action. Whatever those results, the importance lies in deciding ourselves, in being responsible, in doing our own responding and learning. We learn from our "wrong" choices. If we sit on the fence and never decide, we never learn. We need choice, comparison, opposites to clear our way. And by "learning" I refer to becoming more at one with that wonderful, knowing part of ourselves. I believe that part of our humanness lies in developing the intellect, the left brain or masculine mode of thought, before we can fully integrate and balance ourselves to the wisdom of love. Ideally we need to have a fully functioning brain before we can properly carry out the injunctions of unpolarized love.

The Choice to Love, to Co-Create

By choosing to be in a state of love, we begin to be co-creative, using our personal wisdom and experience of positive and negative and our divine core as one. The choice that depends on duality, comparison, and judgment of good and evil disappears—gradually. When we become truly aware of and accept our positive and negative feelings in any situation, tensions dissolve, and we are free to work and play harmoniously. In that freedom, love appears and transforms our choices. We simply *are*. Our intuition is working. At present we perhaps just have inklings of that state of grace.

I have long only wanted "to do God's will," to make the right choice. How do I know what that is? For many years big decisions, such as where I should live, were somehow pointed out to me. For instance, in 1972 when someone told me that on no account must I ever leave Findhorn, I instantly knew that statement was wrong. I turned to my inner guidance, which confirmed my intuition. So I left. Later I wanted to join my friends in Wisconsin, but I somehow knew that the timing was wrong. It was not until I had lived in Ontario for eight years that I felt free to join them. Now the situation has changed again: I have no feeling of right or wrong about living anywhere in particular. I miss the inner knowing, since it imparted a sense of security, the kind of security that people gain from organized church doctrines. I am, I believe, learning to be open to a new relationship with my inner knowing. In the past, a move was somehow made clear to me; now I will be more of a partner in the decision. It is as if my divine self has been carefully guiding me until I am mature enough to be responsible in a new way. I discovered that I had guidance to this effect some twenty-five years ago in a passage from my writings that I shared in chapter 1, on page 31.

Learning to flow with the energies takes us in many directions. We have always drawn to ourselves the situations that are openings for us to learn, to change, but when we allow ourselves to be open, we are more aware of the possibilities and can stop fighting life. The great changes taking place on the planet now, which affect everyone, present wider opportunities. It is a fascinating and interesting time. The principles have always been with us. For example, painting a picture is a matter of continual decision-making, at both a conscious and an unconscious level. If a painter doesn't keep the whole canvas in mind and concentrates only on one area, the painting doesn't come together. Today things will not work unless we keep in mind and heart the whole planet, not just our personal selves.

For creation to occur, it is necessary for there to be attraction and repulsion, negative and positive. Nothing happens contrary to this basic principle. Love cannot love without something to love, something that has been produced out of movement, or the combination and recombination of the elements, the qualities, which arise from the first split into polarities. The split into polarities begins the endless movements that continue to this day, for life consists of change, what might even be called experiment. Love continues to search for how to best function on all levels. Love is intelligent; indeed, polarities are the working out of this intelligence, with the elements as their instruments. Polar opposites run through all creation.

According to the biologist Rupert Sheldrake, creativity arises from the interplay between the negative, matter, the dark, mysterious processes of nature, and the positive, the bright, clear source of ideas reflected in nature. We do not label as good or bad the interplay between polarities in nature, such as electrical and magnetic forces. Nature has no right or wrong pigs or twigs. There is an expansive impulse underlying growth in the universe, while the pull of gravitation holds everything together. There is also a rhythm in polarity, a reversal, so that at certain times positive becomes negative—even the Earth's polarity changes. At a personal level, after childhood we reach a state when a negative emotion, say, of cruelty, becomes repulsive.

Jung believed that the spiritual task of the near future would be to unite the opposites—light and dark, good and evil—which would require quite different attitudes than we have at present. Yet in some older traditions, darkness is the regenerative place from which comes the light, and the Dark Goddess is the Lady of Perpetual Change who gives us something we need by leading us to transformation and regeneration. The Goddess of Regeneration lies within the body of the land; the rebirth of spring cannot come without winter, without death. The guardians of tradition in primal cultures everywhere attempt to balance the dualities of light and dark, men and women, matter and spirit. We can learn from the ancient traditions and link body, mind, and spirit in a new way, a planetary way.

Finding Balance

Planetary changes are bound up with how we view the polarities. In one sense we have labeled our positive or negative feelings about them by our subjective judgments. Attuned or choiceless action doesn't scare me, since I have experienced the angels functioning in that way with joy and purpose. I am fortunate also that I have been led to recognize and accept direction from beyond the personality. I think we have all experienced such direction but have often ignored it and limited ourselves by listening only to certain mindsets.

Some people seem to fear that without personal choice they will lose their freedom. We do lose the so-called freedom of being bound to two opposing powers struggling to solve problems on the level of the problem itself. We can't solve our problems by participating in the strife between the opposites; we must go on to the level where problems are seen as part of wholeness. In dancing, the pair of opposites is always present until the dancer can find the center and then, from the center, move freely.

There are many aspects to polarity. The greater the distance between the two poles, the more powerful the resulting force. The widest range of experience produces the greatest understanding. My method of reaching a meditative state is based on polarity: I focus positively on a high state of consciousness and then become receptive to it, a yearning that evokes a response. There is the body/mind split to be healed. There are the male/female polarities, containing active and receptive processes and differences in abilities in various areas. Certainly the separation of the sexes is responsible for many searches for completion! We are all seeking something, for we live in polarity and always will in this world.

Yet, as is excellently pointed out by the philosopher Ken Wilber in his book *No Boundary*, seeking is itself a boundary, a separating of oneself from something else, a functioning within polarity. By grace we may have mountain-top experiences of atonement with God or with a tree, as I did. Then I found that I could choose to attune to the Beloved at certain times; now the aim is for constant attunement. So I still seek and wonder how best to achieve a continuous consciousness of unity. I find that consciousness at various boundaries, for there I meet differences that give me the opportunity to grow, to incorporate the differences in myself. I know that everyone treads a different path, and because any path may contain a helpful step for me I keep my eyes open.

At the same time, I notice that I can have mean streaks, even murderous or destructive thoughts at times. Are they part of my basic nature? Where do they come from? If I remain identified with my "lower" self and with matter as the only reality, I am restricted to the coagulating power of matter. If I enter a state of love, I am free to function on higher levels. That is wonderful: I become an angel in a realm of harmony. But I am not an angel. I am human, and I want to know how to function in this inharmonious human world of mind and matter and spirit. I need both the "higher" and "lower" to be attuned.

What of my unconscious? According to Jung, unconscious assumptions or opinions are the worst enemy of women. In my experience, women, being responsive beings, are more open than men to other people's assumptions and influences. But we are also all sensitive to an aspect of the collective unconscious—the collective thought world, the mishmash of thoughts expressed day and night by folk all over the planet. We have all experienced in our own thinking or in literature or movies a gamut of impressions and, as humans, can resonate with just about anything. Our thoughts can come from many directions, and we can choose to follow them or not.

Or do "negative" thoughts arise when I am split off from my instinctive physical body? Certainly my body has not been part of my consciousness, and only recently have I begun to realize that I have taken my body completely for granted. My goal is to align the physical, emotional, and mental levels with the spiritual level. Now I consciously relate to my body, sending it love and gratitude—when I remember. I would like to be aware of my instinctiveness, but not subject to it. Just as I want to be conscious of and in control of my cultural behavior, I want to be conscious of and in control of my physical responses.

There is much said and written at present on the need to experience everything, good and bad. While I agree theoretically, some aspects leave me feeling disconnected. For example, I have no desire to experience killing someone. Maybe I have experienced this in the past and learned to make other choices, for we cannot experience everything in one life. As far as I am concerned, each individual enters this life as a special, unique person because of choices and experiences in past lives. Yes, I do desire to know. I have free will to make choices, and I want to understand behavior. We can trust the divine discontent within each of us to bring us the experiences we need and eventually lead to wholeness. I also realize that some "evil" we experience is based on self-preservation or fear, perfectly valid responses to certain situations, which have been magnified in the psychic realms through our usual human swings to excess.

We have populated the thought and feeling worlds with so much abundant life force that these energies and vibrations are strong enough to be powerful entities, kept alive by us. Whatever the cause, whatever tension or imbalance is at the root, we express all sorts and strengths of emotions into the atmosphere, into the astral worlds. Since like attracts like, some emotions coalesce powerfully enough to become an entity, a "devil." An emotion can possess us. How many strange thoughts and feelings do we pick up from the world's reservoir, or, for that matter, from television? As long as we think or feel in terms of vices and virtues, we are open to our own projections of them. Mass projections of feeling are powerful, as evidenced by the way people responded to the speeches of both Gandhi and Hitler. Thinking in polarities and hating something gives energy to what we hate, for what we resist persists. Or we can be friendly to what we hate and to our own weaknesses, not perpetuating their energy by fighting them.

But why do I need to experience these negatives in the first place? Why am I greedy? I believe that we can learn to come to a nonstatic and mutable equilibrium, which is perfect freedom, by knowing what is on both sides of the balance, what the poles of receptivity and expression are. The areas in which I am out of sync are simply the areas in which I am finding balance. Some time I will honor my body more and my desire for sweet things less. Through greed I learn to choose less excess, because if I continue on the path of excess I get into trouble, perhaps even addiction, and begin a long course of learning. In my understanding of this process I presuppose many chances for choice, in a universe of the God of love. I can stop feeling guilty about my greed by accepting myself as I am. I'm still working toward this goal, though at present I choose a chocolate-filled world! I even know that we can use the experience of pain, restriction, and discipline as a means of gaining greater consciousness and fulfillment. I know that pure observation and recognition of a hatred, an anxiety, a sadness reveals its nature and brings a freedom that leads to healing and emancipation. We have our choices; we can decide to love.

Jung wrote that one does not become enlightened by imagining figures of light, but by making the darkness conscious. In other words, when I chose to stop resisting and condemning myself, the Beloved was there. Truth, love, God, is always present, hidden behind whatever situation is necessary for us to learn through, until we find that presence in complete acceptance of what is, without judgment. This attitude may seem too condoning of evils like murder. But what can I do about a murder or the act of murder except make my own choices? Being fearful about it only adds fear to the world—and puts money into the hands of people who live on our fears. Nonjudgment at least doesn't add any psychic power to the world reservoir; it allows what is to stand forth more clearly. Judgment is like a wall surrounding events. We can love the murderer without condoning the act of murder.

Taken a step further, sending love to the murderer might help—goodness knows he or she needs help. My stresses and tensions regarding missing airplane flights taught me that sending forth nonjudgmental love to a person or situation can have deeply powerful results. That love is beyond the realms of opposites. Occasionally, I have felt moved to express such love when watching the news on television, directing it to the situation in question while remaining aware of the crises but completely nonjudgmental as to good and bad. That "neutrality" is not passive or static; its freedom is powerfully creative and enables love to gain access anywhere. The Spindrift research, which experimented with sending directed and nondirected prayers to growing beans, found that nondirected (Thy will be done) prayer was more effective.[1]

Our negative emotions can show us the way to love. For instance, one day at the airport I was told my flight had been delayed two hours. I waited two hours and then was told there would be another two-hour delay. Since my flight was only two hours long, I became annoyed and nastily complained to the desk attendant. Then I realized it wasn't her fault, and I felt guilty. That made me determine not to be nasty anymore. In this case the guilt was a help. I perceive more and more that negative emotions, when accepted, somehow change the situation and initiate us into a new awareness, a new balance.

True balance stands at the point between the extremes of anything, but we need to understand and employ the extremes. For the fullest range of tone in paint, the extremes of black and white are used, not just the gray that is their balance. For the richest life, the fullest range of emotions are experienced, not a neutral place of little feeling. We employ the extremes, the polarities, from the creative center that sees the purpose or beauty of any characteristic, whether of paint, emotion, music, or so on. The true equilibrium of anything is not a rigid two-halves equality; it is more a holy trinity. On the physical level it

---

1. Dossey, Larry. *Recovering the Soul: A Scientific and Spiritual Approach.* New York: Bantam Doubleday, 1989.

can be more like the Japanese *ikebana* method of flower arrangement, relating three components to each other in infinite ways. In China, the dynamic of *Chi* (the basic energy of the universe) is balance. A Taoist proverb says: "If you have a disease, which you want to find and cure, seek your center." That center is not static. It is not a form of inertia, but rather finding and keeping to a razor's edge between diametrically opposed contraries in a changing world. It is the boundary where we meet the differences that give us opportunities. At this moment in history, we must find a balance between annihilation and transformation, and we have vast energies at our disposal. It is a time to see the folly of remaining at one extreme, and to understand that deeper levels of consciousness are contained in diversity. In the union of positive and negative we have creativity. Finding balance is never dull and calls for acute observation and awareness. Accepting the spectrum of life results in freedom. It is *lila*, the divine play. We play with the binding power of the cosmos, called love, the most powerful force of which we are conscious.

Role of Negativity

I began to see a purpose in negative feelings and to understand the meaning behind the Buddhist recognition of the need for suffering and conflict as a path of growth, a cosmic plan to bring us into wholeness. Without destruction, life could not exist. Negative emotions like depression can take us to an emptiness that makes room for new birth. I had a passive friend who needed anger to spur her to take action. We all know that physical pain draws our attention to something that is not functioning properly, giving us the opportunity to respond and heal. Negative emotions are experiences and conditions to help us grow, bringing us choices and opportunities.

We need them as the chick needs to break the shell before it emerges; otherwise, it is too weak to live. Our negative emotions and actions are gifts. These gifts have been listed as sins, vices, forms of bondage, and, unfortunately, at present we have become so unbalanced that we have drawn a plethora of negative forces to us. Our poisoning of the air, the land, the sea, is teaching us to behave differently. With understanding and love, we can change the imbalance. There is no new life or evolution without destruction; destruction is creation in another realm. There is Beauty, there is the Beast.

At the same time, it is important to recognize that a realization of our faults is an aid only when we are committed to improving ourselves or tapping into the inner life; otherwise it is a burden.

In *The Universe Is a Green Dragon*, the physicist Brian Swimme, citing cultural historian Thomas Berry as his inspiration, presents a unique view. He writes that beauty and allurement are the root of all evil activity. For example, nuclear weapons are the result of human fascination with the cosmos; tapping the awesome sources of power is irresistible to the human mind. The great mystery is not violence, but beauty. Books that honor the usefulness and the positive role of the negative are appearing from various sources, including shamans and particularly psychologists. They write of how physical and emotional pain is the root of changes in our viewpoints, how following our emotions leads to the source, love. They indicate that our cultural assumptions are changing. From these books I understand more clearly that we in the West still embrace the scientific, either/or Aristotelian logic that leads to an extreme dualism where inner unity disappears. On the whole, Western culture is a example of the idea that good may exist without evil, light without darkness.

Attuning to a Negative

For years and years I did not even try to attune to a "negative" angel: I found no such energy in the angelic realms. I have always maintained that there are no dark angels, though powerful dark beings do exist in the psychic realms as embodiments of our human negative emotions, such as fear. I still maintain this to be true. But I could attune to what I have called the "positives," though it is equally true that there are no angels with just positive qualities. We simply don't have words for what angels are, the seed of both positive and negative. Nevertheless it irked me that angels were considered only to be positive; I felt something was being left out. Was my lack of desire to contact a dark angel simply a result of judging the negative as bad? Eventually I did try the negative approach, using cruelty as my example; at first I felt a sense of sadness within myself and in the "cruelty angel"—making me realize that I was not in the angelic realm, in which positive and negative are one. Delving more deeply into love, I experienced a transformation. I was aware of cruelty and kindness twirling around each other, equally loving and equally loved.

As with attuning to the four elements, I needed a great deal of love to experience the transformation of positive and negative and to know that in the world of unity, cruelty and kindness are one essence. Like most of us, I react against negativity and try not to choose it. I had always experienced wholeness through what I called the positive. As the popular song of the 1940s tells us, "Accentuate the positive, eliminate the negative." Now another view has arisen, which calls for more love and no judgment, a participation in the full spectrum of life.

Full participation can be, and possibly always is, painful. In the 1970s the fact that dolphins were hacked off nets or otherwise destroyed because they got in the way of tuna fishing became common knowledge. I heard such stories, but I didn't want to know about them. I didn't want to hear about cruelty. Eventually I told myself to stop being an ostrich, hiding away from life. So I watched a documentary on the subject. It hurt so much that I rolled on the floor in real agony. I didn't hate it; I just accepted it and its result. It was a deep experience, so profound that I felt it helped in some way. I was experiencing a depth, without adding any unhelpful energy to the world. I was not denying or supporting. I believe that unless we let ourselves feel such intense emotions, we are not truly taking part in the human experience.

My own biases, or personality-based projections, came out in another way. I have always hated the color black. I love the rainbow colors but not black. I would never wear black, though it didn't bother me if other people wore it. At one point I went through my apartment and eliminated everything black, even taking out lines around the mats in picture frames. This resulted in a sensation of floating, but I liked it. Then life led me to a job as a hotel receptionist, where it was customary to wear black. I quietly wore charcoal gray, for it was unbearable to me to wear black. I got away with the gray for a time, until I was told that black was obligatory. I purchased a black cashmere twin set, hoping that the beautiful feel of the cashmere would reconcile me to the color. On the very first day that I wore it, I received a telegram saying that my beloved father had died. This event more than confirmed me in my hatred of black. More recently, my interest in polarities has helped me recognize that my deep reaction against black was a great example of bias and attachment on my part, acceptable as a choice but not as an emotional reaction. I don't want to be reactionary. So I have been wearing black, to see if I can learn to like it—which I do occasionally! Of course, when I'm truly loving I can love it.

In our human world, the negative forces are powerfully out of balance and have enormous influence. In the emotions we express, negative ones are more obvious than in the past; they are being given weight. They fascinate us, and in the press and on television, what is negative is news and interesting. What is positive is dull. We can empathize with sorrow; joy can seem misplaced and annoying in our calamitous world. And in this way we continue to add energy to the negative, until something changes us. A positive aspect of all this emphasis on the negative is that it brings the negative into focus, which is a step forward. Hidden motivations cannot be dealt with. In this context one could say that good is the active power created through struggling against an adversary.

Different Ideas, Different Lessons

Generally speaking, in the East a sense of community is developed, in the West a sense of individuality. The Eastern world upholds the ideal principle of the whole, that is, the group or state, as more important than the individual. In the West the development of the individual has been given emphasis. Selfhood with freedom has had no meaning in the Orient, and our selfish materialism is considered something to repudiate. Eastern thought and Western thought have different worldviews. The West teaches that evil is to be fought and overcome. The East considers that ignorance, repulsion, and negativity are areas to be understood as part of life. Since there is no life without the positive and the negative, attraction and repulsion, ignorance exists when we don't recognize the role of both sides in life. Now as the planet shrinks and we realize that we all live in an interrelated system, these seemingly contradictory views are coming together. It is a time for people to learn from and appreciate both community and individuality, and to express differences while understanding and respecting their value. Of course it is *maya* (illusion), now confirmed by science, to believe that what the senses comprehend is real and solid. Recognizing the reality of the spiritual level, and yet at the same time fully appropriating and enjoying the experiences the senses offer, is truly intelligent and loving. All of life is to be loved.

At different stages of human growth, at different levels of awareness, various processes have their parts to play. First we are protected, surrounded, and encouraged by our cultural definitions and the injunctions of polarities. When we see beyond what are at first helpful limitations, we begin to make the choices that move us individually. We gain spiritual strength, aided as always by our soul's surfacing as much as we will let it. Life helps us choose, gives us every opportunity to become more aware, even though we resist most of the time. Anything horrible we find generally mirrors some aspect of our consciousness back to us. We become aware of our female and male functions, when to be receptive and when to be assertive, and use them appropriately. According to Alan Watts, a philosopher of the 1960s, life is problematic so long as it seems that there is a real choice between the opposites. True integrity therefore lies in understanding that it is simply impossible to take sides, except in play or illusion. If the game is won, life ceases. Many archetypes imply this game: the Trickster, the Divine Juggler of the Bhagavad Gita, the Fool of the Tarot, and so on. Is the answer to not take life seriously? For life is not a matter of life or death; life is a matter of life and death, and ultimately there is nothing to dread.

Three Stages: Instinct, Choice, Love

As I see it, humans pass through three main stages. First, as portrayed in the story of the garden of Eden, we are purely instinctive and have no choice. Second, we gain the ability to choose, free will, through which we become self-conscious and develop the intellect. This stage is symbolized by the tree of the knowledge of good and evil. Third, as embodied in the tree of life, we choose a greater whole, the "choiceless choice" mentioned by Krishnamurti, the allurement of love, of beauty, that takes us back to God.

Eventually there is but one way, not that of good or bad but that of nonjudgmental love, the quality at the foundation of every pair of opposites. We can be attuned to love sufficiently to stop choosing between the opposites, to stop following the intellectual mind. I experienced the problem of the intellect continually interrupting me when I first began to meditate, and the Beloved asked me not to let the critical, analyzing mind be my boss, but instead to attune to the universal mind. Through the years I grew better at that. Now I am at a place where, though the intellect may still hold sway over me in action, I recognize it. I can change and I can become better at loving—for the Beloved is here. With that love we begin living out our human destiny, loving and lifting up our world.

Choosing love does not mean that we lose all discrimination or cease acting on behalf of the whole or of any particular situation. More clearly than ever we are open to recognizing inequalities, cruelties, harshness, and so on, and to taking any action for which we can be responsible. We need to follow our inner integrity with greater faithfulness than ever. We commit ourselves more deeply to the whole, to the planet. We accept the beautiful spiritual philosophy of the East but bring it to the physical level, which the East often ignores. Conversely, we take action on the material level but from a spiritual viewpoint, which the West generally overlooks.

To repeat, love is the quality that encompasses all the power and strengths of positive concern and of the deepest receptive learning. With love at the center, the world is essentially the same, yet completely transformed. Love's wholeness includes the negative and extends beyond light and dark. Anger has helpful aspects and can be constructively channeled. Love embraces the whole; those who are cruel are reacting to something that has driven them to an extreme, and because love, or God, is within them, they will learn—sometime, somewhere. Love and life never give up. Peace and clarity begin with recognizing that there is conflict, both inner and outer, and if we suppress hate, we never find love. The deep, suffering kind of emotions are what teach us, move us, open the door to answers. The actions that we take from hate, anger, or cruelty derive from our "normal" state of separation from our true core, abetted by our cultural backgrounds, the human condition of the world. Love runs the gamut of all qualities and accepts the sacred in everything, ignoring appearances. Jung said that the developed consciousness stands between the opposites, for the personality cannot identify completely with either good or evil; we swim between the opposites until we reconcile them. Although tears of joy and tears of sorrow are similar, according to endocrinologist Deepak Chopra, each has a different chemical makeup.

Choice to Change

In following the evolutionary dynamism within us, we have learned by trial and error, and at the moment the error is gigantic enough for us to notice it and make a change. In developing our mental creativity, we have ignored our right-brain functions, the feminine and nurturing aspect of ourselves, and the resulting world certainly appears to be in a mess. With that dynamism, and the realization of the consequences of our actions in mistreating the planet, we are learning that we must change, we must act differently. The angels believe we can do it in time, and I would hate to contradict them! We won't stop making advances in technology, but we must stop believing in the illusion that technology is the cure.

Awakening love within us is a matter of focus and choice, of learning the pragmatic power of the Christian commandment to love ourselves and our neighbor, whether friends or enemies. It is choosing to align the personality with the soul level. Following that path gives us a broad focus and widens us to embrace the planet. We will keep on being hurt until we love, personally and impersonally.

Moving beyond the pairs of opposites and yet functioning in this world of polarity is to live as the angels do, with the same basic qualities from which polarity emerges but in the context of this nitty-gritty world. In our unity beyond the splintered parts of ourselves, we find the real. We have a task more difficult than that of our angelic kin—to live and experience the heights and depths that humanity has probed as well as the beautiful and balanced world of nature, and to maintain our balance. It is an incredible task, but we are geared to play our planetary role by living into our divine natures. Everything in life, including our judgment of polarities and the ecological crisis, is moving us to this growth, and we need not suffer or create suffering any longer. It is time to be more fully human. Yet paradoxically, to be fully human is to love intensely, and that intensity often feels like suffering!

The angels alerted me to this human task in 1971:

♋

When you, humans, rise to your true estate and sound your note as clearly and purely as the bird that welcomes the dawn, all worlds will stop, listen, and learn, for your note will be their goal. We are speaking this from the world of the angels, those who have not left wholeness and who are trusted to wield power throughout the cosmos. Now we are your teachers, messengers, and exemplars of how to live in a world that is one, and that is easy for us because our world is one and even our form can be one when this is inwardly necessary.

For you we have provided the means for life's finest expression, to be many and yet one in the most difficult and challenging conditions. As you meet the challenge—which you must in the divine wisdom—we marvel at our handiwork. Then it is your turn to be teacher, for the Love of God walks on Earth in your consciousness, and all life is included, and the Love of God reaches out to itself in other planets and other systems.

As you reach out to those distant worlds, remember we have been there first, we who have not the limitations of time and space and who control the forces of the universe. You may call this energy positive and negative, even label it good and evil, but when the fruit of the tree of knowledge has been digested, you will know that all is one. You will be proof of it, having emerged from the wars of the opposites to unity. In your knowledge you will know as we do not know. You will have our consciousness and more, and qualities to rise to greater tasks. Your estate will be vast and will grow, and we will grow because of it. As we all grow, we expand and yet become one.

So let us be your teachers and share our joy and limitlessness. Then let us go on as you share your seasoned love, and all life rejoices and returns to the One.

This does not mean, in this world of polarity, that we no longer suffer, and yet it does mean that! It depends on our love, our attitude. I experienced a wonderful example of this when I was being given treatment for sluggish circulation. The treatment hurt; thumbs were pressed so hard into me at various places that I thought I couldn't stand it. I felt forced to do something. I decided to accept the thumb pressures as coming from God, whom I knew as love. Immediately the pain ceased, and I had a wonderful, painless session, and the practitioner also had a wonderful experience. When we stop resisting and accept, love is free to enter, and suffering is over.

I used to think that in the future there would be no darkness, and the necessary contrast would be in different colors, rainbow colors. But such a world would be one without great depth—light shines brightly only in the dark. A world without much contrast would be insipid. Yes, that is the world of the angels, but our human world can be richer, one the angels cannot emulate. To love in the darkness is our human prerogative.

I now can accept the dark side, and acceptance imparts a freedom that makes room for love to arise anywhere. But I am still learning to be unlimited enough to *love* the dark side. I know deeply that such a love is possible. I am learning the value of the dark, which gives us depth, magnitude, and intensity and goes beneath the surface to puncture righteousness and old patterns. It is even possible to love physical pain, as I have shared. Without experiencing suffering, humans would be hard-hearted, insensitive to the consequence of life, cut off from the soul. Seeing suffering or imperfection also draws out heart qualities. When we love, they change. The gift of incarnation on Earth has encompassed millions of years of light and darkness, at first without suffering, I believe. Then, as the organs of sensitivity evolved and self-knowing became possible, suffering became a way to gain awareness. And, as awareness and love grow, suffering turns back to the source, love, as it is with the One. Eventually we do not just love, we *are* love.

This evolution calls for nonjudgment, which is my undertaking. Our judgments have been essential to our choices. They have been a way to meet our reality, and making correct choices give us self-esteem. Our first lessons as babies teach us to judge, to choose between what is good or bad for us. Choices arise through comparison, exercises of the intellect. In the vastness of life, the intellect chooses its patterns, judging and comparing everything, finding continuity through those choices. Yet every judgment links us with our past and keeps us from the freedom of the present. According to the healer Deepak Chopra, every judgment gives signals to the body, a signal of discomfort; nonjudgment is silence for the mind and bliss for the body. Only without judgment can we be ourselves, without pain or pleasure. Judgment and choices are necessary phases in our development, so we don't need to feel guilty about them. Now is the time to be nonjudgmental and find the freedom where love is.

Exercise:

Do the Krishnamurti exercise: Think of a fault, some characteristic in yourself that you don't like and want to rid yourself of or change, a negativity, failure, or suffering. Then look at it without judgment, without any opinion, without expectation, without thought of change, without comfort. Accept it without any idea of right or wrong or of how it fits in. Just see it. It's a difficult exercise, because many of us who would venture to do it are inclined to see that the difficulties we list may indeed have taught us something. But that is still a judgment, a movement of thought. The point is to have no judgment, having already judged!

⌘ CHAPTER THREE

LOVE'S QUALITIES

⌘

*We are the embodiment of all myth, for our qualities encompass all
human striving on Earth. We change; therefore we are the past and
future as well as the present. We inspire, for that is our nature. We
have the job of spreading the creative God-qualities on Earth. We
are called the Builders; we are the builders not only of form but
also of realms and majesty, which are immanent in everything.
Like all myth, the reality of it has to be born through expression on
Earth. How is a myth brought to birth? Partly by building on
what has already been born—and there is nowhere in the world
where there is not something to be mythic about.*

— The Devas, September 1977

Attuning to the Qualities of the Plant World

For the first ten years of my meditating, my attunement was
to God the Beloved, apart from various telepathic contacts.
Evidently I was meant to branch into a specific part of life, for
in May l963 my inner guidance told me that I had a job to do.
I was to harmonize with the essence of nature, and all nature
has an ensouling intelligence, from planets to vegetables. After
trying to overcome my belief that it was ridiculous for a vegetable to be intelligent, I chose to experiment with the garden

pea, my favorite to eat. This plant was familiar to me from my father's garden, and I now realize that the outer form of anything gives some indication of its inner essence. The word "essence" was familiar to me, for I had been attuning to my own essence for ten years. That day, in a powerful meditative state, I tried to imagine what would be the essence, the kernel, of the unique form, scent, color, and taste of the pea. Focusing strongly on that question, I received a flow of intelligence from within similar to what I receive from God, and, as before, I put the experience into words. I recognized that I was communicating with the soul of the species, a planetary intelligence in charge of all garden peas in the world. In fact, I was connecting with the builders of form responsible for the processes by which manifestation takes place. The only word I had for such an energy was "angel." Because in my culture angels have a particular form, drawn from medieval art, and because what I was contacting was a formless energy field, I generally thereafter used the word "deva," which is Sanskrit for "shining one." I had no preconceived images of a deva. After my initial contact with the soul of the pea, a conscious cooperation with this invisible world evolved, out of which the Findhorn garden developed. I received answers to questions on gardening, and by following the suggestions we grew tasty food prolifically.

Each plant required a delicate attention to its unique vibration. The contact deepened, particularly after we had imbibed some of the angelic principles and did not need to ask so many questions. After four years we introduced flowers into the garden. With them I could concentrate more on inner attunement, and became delightedly aware of the diverse energies, the gossamer feel of each. Through this contact with the soul of each species, I was experiencing different qualities of love, of the sacred, expressed through the variety of nature. I tried to express the contrasting perceptions in words. For instance, from the bouncy vibrations of the pansy I wrote:

⌘

We bounded into the garden quite determinedly! In any case, we get along with man more than other plants and are well looked after, cultivated and appreciated, and the very picking of us is good for us because we like producing. We are natural givers. We love the rain and the sun and the earth and the air. Perhaps the word "love" gives you a wrong meaning; we are part of the rain and the sun and the earth and the air. All of us are; you are, too, not just your physical bodies; all your bodies are manifestations in their levels of these elements.

From the quieter energy of the rhododendron, I wrote:

⌘

Vivid and somber, sunshine and rain, and over all a great love for being, a tenacity and exclusiveness. We settle in wherever we can and get down to the business of being. We thank you for bringing us into the garden; we thank all who have allowed us a roothold and life through the country, for we do love to settle.

Understanding Other Dimensions

These inner attunements held great joy; I loved them and felt at home. They helped train me in sensitive response to different qualities. They also helped me notice more, identify and value the variegated shapes of nature, the differences in leaf, in petal, in trees, in everything. I also began to attune to the mineral and animal worlds.

At first the presences themselves did not seem loving; they seemed rather remote, even cold. It was not until eight years after my initial contact with them that I realized that one can resonate to or understand only what one has in oneself. I wondered if the devas seemed unloving because *I* was unloving. I asked them if this was so, and they explained that they swam in a sea of love, that their love was universal, not limited and directed like human love. They became one with what they loved. I had expected a personal love focused on me. This different understanding helped me appreciate the vastness of an impersonal love that included everything. In my experience, angelic love is not emotional, and angels do not react but remain centered in love. From my inner core, from God, I received both a personal and an impersonal love.

The inner worlds were becoming ever more real to me, though they were not tangible to my five senses. Years earlier I had attended the School of the Natural Order, founded by the American master Vitvan. I realized from his teaching that our senses only interpret reality. For example, we interpret our bodies as solid, but they are 99 percent space, our atoms being a distance from each other similar to the planets of our solar system. An airplane propeller in motion cannot be seen, yet it is devastatingly tangible to an arm put in its way. Now, what I had learned as intellectual facts became real through experience. By attuning to different dimensions, I was strengthening my sensitivities, and developing intuition, a sense of knowing.

Qualities as Intelligent and as Presented in Mythology

One day, I was asked from within to attune to serenity. That seemed a strange request, but I did it and, to my amazement, found an intelligence communicating with me. That a quality itself could have intelligence was a new idea to me. In a rush of illumination, I realized that the gods and goddesses of all cultures are based on energies, on qualities like serenity, which we have personified, named, used as symbols, and told stories about throughout history. As personified deities, they represent qualities with which we humans resonate—our virtues and vices. Each of us is unique in that we have a different combination of these energies. They are the forces behind our thinking, feeling, and action, lying deep in the core of us and coming into play in our minds, emotions, and actions. The great Christian winged angels, whether we deem them comforting or archaic, are our representations of the same energies. We have given them lustrous names like Raphael ("God has healed"), Uriel ("God is my light"), or Michael ("who is like God," a guardian) that reflect those energies.

I began to find a new understanding of what in the past were considered "the gods." I had been fond of the Greek myths; now I had discovered for myself that the gods are based on actual living, intelligent force fields. I no longer felt superior to what I had previously considered to be superstitious nonsense, the old beliefs and religions of primitive and previous cultures. I realized that they were based on actual forces that are part of our planet, part of our universe, seen through the understanding of the humans at the time. We too are all these energies. We each automatically incorporate and reflect these force fields in our souls, consciously or unconsciously.

My newfound illumination that the gods and goddesses of all cultures are the names and symbols we give to the powerful forces influencing human and natural actions, so vivid that they have been personified throughout history, led me to new explorations. In Greek mythology the gods produced many children. I wondered simplistically which quality begat another. The Muses are the children of Zeus, father of the gods, and Mnemosyne, Memory, and they preside over literature, art, and science. The metaphor seemed accurate: the higher creative energy, or father, seeded the mental faculty of memory to produce works of inspiration in different fields. Pallas Athena, goddess of wisdom, sprang mature from the head of Zeus. Other children of Zeus are themselves gods, or else mortal heroes. I was fascinated by the apparent appropriateness of the genesis of these archetypes. The Greeks seemed to have instinctively understood patterns of behavior. I found similar patterns presented in the folk stories of other cultures.

Qualities as Images

People often say that we communicate with other worlds or dimensions through the imagination. The word "imagination" to me meant imaging or picturing something, and that was not how I experienced other dimensions. What I was aware of was not a picture, not a form, but a quality, an energy, an essence intelligently communicating to me meanings, which I abstracted according to my understanding and translated into words. The words we have for describing anything are based on the world as we see it through the senses, with our added emotional and mental reactions, which are also based on the senses. We describe a quality as, say, "gentle as cotton fluff," or "gentle as the tickle of a feather," or "soft as water." There are thousands of different gradations of color in paint, and these, too, we name. One particular green, for instance, is called "nocturnal sea." It is difficult to depict quality, though it is very "real." It is part of our human nature to name things, our way of expressing consciousness.

I believe that in the past, people were generally clairvoyant, that is, they were open to seeing other dimensions and might see the qualities as color or as patterns, like the pattern of metal filings arranged by a magnet. They were perhaps aware of the force fields that I have termed angelic, translating their perceptions according to the cultural understandings of the time. The fear and impotence that our ancestors felt in the presence of the power of nature and of the unknown influenced how they imagined and pictured everything, including their gods. The god images of primitive cultures often look frightening. I believe that this clairvoyance waned or vanished as mental faculties were developed. Then people gained greater control of nature, and their god images became less frightening and more what we call normal and beautiful. In the Greek culture our Western conception of beauty became defined and ideally sculpted in statues. In fact, when photos or drawings of modern Caucasian faces are laid on top of each other, the composite face is that of a Greek god.

Although our Western ideal of physical facial beauty has changed little in two thousand years, I believe our consciousness has changed. We have lost the clairvoyance of ancient times and gained independent thought through growth and experience. Our minds became dominant. We did a considerable job of mental development in the West, dispensing with God and the gods and enthroning reason and science, to the great benefit of technical improvement and the great detriment of the planet's environment. When we lost belief in the Christian angels, we deprived ourselves of the aid we can receive when we ask for their help.

Qualities as Archetypes

Carl Jung perceived the gods as archetypes of the unconscious. I have no training in the Jungian approach, but I gather that he recognized the Greek gods as personifications of fundamental characteristics that, although they are unique to each individual, are universally present in all of us and in the collective unconscious. If there indeed exist in human beings certain psychic and behavioral forms that are both unique and universally present in everyone, one could assume that we have the potential to use them all. According to physicist David Bohm, "What the cosmos is doing as we dialogue is to change its ideas of itself. Through us the universe deciphers and changes its own being. Humans may be realizing a role in nature once reserved for the gods."

The mythologist Joseph Campbell also brought the value of the stories of the gods to our attention. Throughout his life he tried to forge a kind of unified field theory of inner energies, an amalgam of myth, religion, science, and art, the personification of which he called the gods. He explained the role of mythology in our lives and splendidly stretched our faculties to understand lost meanings. For him, myths and rites are attempts to control society and make it accord with nature. Myths are metaphors opening us up to the world so that it becomes more understandable and uplifting; in this context deities are personifications of ourselves. Campbell went beyond traditional scholarship into spiritual and psychological views of mythology, saying that the transcendent reality referred to by saints and shamans could be directly experienced, and that what mystics called cosmic consciousness is nothing less than a personal encounter with the gods. I understand that Campbell also believed that myth is a function of biology, that what energies we have are determined by the organs of the body. I see the same biological connection the other way around: each individual is integrated structurally and functionally from a certain background or force field.

From many viewpoints, mythological stories can be of endless help. If the actions of the gods and of humans are based on the same qualities, lasting myths are the garnering of the traditional wisdom of the race. Our knowledge of human nature is being expanded by our study of the stories of the gods. More important, we can work directly with the energies we call the gods, whose powers encompass all our needs. They are not mere abstractions. Certainly I was expanded when I reached the energy level I call angelic. I realized that because I could experience joy and resonate with the joy of the angelic realm, I, too, must have the quality of joy in my makeup. This held true for all the angelic qualities, and it followed that we humans have endowments similar to those of the angels; we are part angel. Angels remain clear and pure at their undifferentiated level, as do our pure souls.

Seed Qualities

In one respect it seemed that my experiences were somewhat different from most mythical accounts, in that to me, for instance, the Angel of Joy and the Angel of Sorrow are one angel. Complementary opposites are still one in angelic dimensions. The angelic energy field contains the seed of psychic, emotional, and mental substance before the essence is manifested through polarization. Incidentally, reaching those essence levels in each contact with the angels was a wonderful training in awakening to the essence level in myself, in practicing wholeness.

If, as I understand it, qualities form patterns at all levels, then all forms, including our bodies, reflect them. They are the energies from which all creation derives. We spend our lives learning from their combinations and recombinations. They are the treasures that do not rust, that we take with us always. There is an evolutionary dynamism within us that urges us to become increasingly aligned with these qualities. They create us, and we constantly express and recreate them, for our creations are the expression of their energies. Creative impulses constantly flow into the world both from other realms and from us as humans, giving new impulses and shaping reality.

Quality influences life in various subtle ways that we don't often recognize. For instance, I have heard that if hunters go out with guns but with no intention of killing, animals don't avoid them as they do when there is the intent to kill. I recall recognizing invisible energies when driving along a skyway in Chicago. I began to be afraid; fear was in the air, no doubt coming from the fearful conditions in that part of the city. Working in the garden with a loving attitude is, according to the nature angels, as important as the work itself. Evidently, the intention behind an action defines its effects on certain lasting, or "higher," levels, though not always in the arena of finite forms. The quality of our thoughts and feelings determines the level on which we create or get a response. This view ties in with that of Tibetan medicine, which holds that the root causes of disease are ignorance, desire, or hatred.

Gaining Access to Soul Qualities in Our Daily Lives

My attunements with the angels were experiences that heightened in me qualities helpful in everyday living, just as my attunements with the Beloved did. Delicate though they were, each contact was a strengthening of some unknown part of myself, a sensitivity that could now find its place in life and was an aspect of love. Of course, I continued with my usual inner attunements to the sacred, and they encouraged me to continue with the devic ones. The God attunements somehow touched deeper and richer qualities than those of the plants, minerals, or animals, which were more specific, more particularized.

Many people gain access to the soul level of qualities, or the Absolute, through using various dynamic images that have resonance for them, such as saints, gods, angels, archetypes, or ancestors. Others access them via Otherworld journeys or vision quests, or through psychology, astrology, numerology, and so forth. What matters is what works for each person. There are as many paths to God as there are people, and we have the freedom to choose what seems right to us or what we love.

When I began to give workshops and had groups attune to the souls of various plant, mineral, and animal species, we reached these qualities directly. In our ordinary lives we can also call on the traits needed to solve our problems via the god or animal representing those qualities, as did the Homeric Greeks and the American Indians. The same method is just as valid today. Any power is available to us, for we incorporate all life; we are the microcosm of the macrocosm.

At first, I used joy as an example for an exercise. Somehow, when there were so many terrible problems in the world, making it difficult to experience rapture, joy did not seem relevant. Courage seemed more appropriate in such hazardous times. I myself sometimes used the archetypal symbol, calling on Mars for courage. It was fun to do it that way, to imagine an ancient warrior. Actually, our aim was to *be* courage or whatever quality was chosen, not just to think about it. The more we resonate with what have been called the virtues, the more likely we are to incorporate and express them. In our exercises, most of us succeeded in evoking the suggested area of ourselves and felt better and more prepared for the trials of everyday life.

Love as the Seedbed

As I conducted more workshops, I had the opportunity to delve increasingly deeper into each quality we invoked. Always

I found love at the base. If one has enough love, one has enough courage, enough endurance, enough patience, enough willpower, and so on, to deal with any situation. I began to recognize at a deep level that God *is* love. I could liken love, God, to white light, which can be split into myriad rainbow colors. I began to perceive creation as love separating into the different qualities.

The universe is so vast, and there are so many ways of approaching its mysterious immensity, that the simple statement that God, the energy behind all that is, is love, seems inadequate, biased, and futile, especially in this culture, where love is most often perceived as a sexual force. Whatever the original creative force was, that One must have differentiated and become many. Most traditions postulate a primary energy, which then manifests as "stepped down" energy currents known as the elements. In China, Taoism postulated the Supreme Ultimate, which generated two primary forms, *yin* (the feminine), and *yang* (the masculine). Another perception is of the various trinities, and I know best the trinity of Will, Love/Wisdom, and Creative Intelligence, as expounded by Alice Bailey. Threesomes are creative ensembles. For this planet I see the greatest of these three aspects as love, it being the prime quality sponsoring will and intelligence and producing the necessary balance sometimes called the Christ. I realize that the quality termed will is very much part of the mystery of unfolding life and is particularly difficult for humans to understand. The Sufi teacher Inayat Khan said that willpower is love. There may be other universes that function on a different system in which love is not the prime manifesting energy, but for this planet it seems that love is our goal, our practice, our destiny.

To me, love is the seedbed of all the qualities, the substance of the building bricks of the universe. The seminal qualities of the universe are registered through polarization at all levels of life, in the mental and emotional levels, and manifested farther "down" in the physical realm. These are the energies that give birth to the stars, the planets, everything in the cosmos. In humans we see them expressed most readily in the psychic or emotional realms, as our different personality characteristics. All of us have these seed qualities in us in differing proportions. Our particular mix is what makes us unique. Each culture has a different amalgam, and we develop different qualities at different times in our evolution. On our soul level we encounter the essence of these qualities more directly, for the angelic realm lives closer to essence, not having taken on form as we have. According to Rudolf Steiner, the spiritual teacher of the philosophy known as anthroposophy, God used the orders of the angels as body and limbs to create and maintain the world, in the same way that a person makes use of arms and hands to work on Earth. Or one could say that humans and angels share the same energy fields, albeit humans do so unconsciously (though we are now expanding our awareness). Some people are becoming global and holistic in their perspective, like the angels. Both humans and angels are mythic beings.

The angelic world is the builder not merely of outer form in nature, but also of inner form, of our emotional and mental worlds. All patterns come from the subtle energies that we know best as qualities. One definition of angels is the images or expressions through which the essences and energy forces of God can be transmitted. Christianity lists these essences as virtues, positive qualities to aspire to. As I have said, my experience of them was that they contained both negativity and positivity, yin and yang. Our "virtues" I envision as an equilibrium between too much and too little, a balanced, nonstatic state where creativity sparks.

Potentialities

To me the concept of the potentiality of qualities has immense implications. It is another way of seeing that each of us is a co-creator with the sacred. Any of us can resonate with the quality of joy or sorrow, friendliness or unfriendliness, or any of the pairs of opposites, because we all have these qualities within us and also the developing capacity and power to choose wholeness. We are each the universe in miniature, with all potential, yet each unique in our different combinations of all the essences. In our physical forms we are the outcome of millions of years of evolution. In our inner selves we are creative planetary beings. We are here in a world to unfold that creativity in different ways, having all the necessary capacities to do so. We are the one and the many. Through science, we know that nothing is affected without affecting everything. Every individual motion is also universal motion, intelligence acting.

Everything in the universe is alive with a spark of divinity, and the reflections or representations of this divinity have generally been expressed in terms of the powers of nature. Mysticism sees being as a wholeness from which parts devolve without losing the identity of the original whole, not unlike a hologram. Modern science perceives creation as a formula relating matter and energy. As a mystic, I see all forms as having consciousness; the physicist states that all forms are interconnected energies, and the sciences are beginning to find consciousness in matter, in molecules, in DNA.

Manifestation

One view of how different qualities take shape in form was explained to me early on by the Apple Deva:

⌘

From the seed idea, a pattern of force issues from the center, passed on by silent ranks of angels, silent and still because the idea is too unformed and unfixed to endure any but the most exacting care. Down and out it comes, growing in strength and size, becoming brighter in pattern until eventually, still in the care of the outmost great angel, it scintillates and sounds. Its force field is steady and brilliant. Then the pattern is passed to the makers of form, the elementals, who come and give themselves to clothe that pattern. Remember, this is a process; the pattern is everywhere apparent in the ethers, held by the angels and made manifest by the energy of the elements through the ministration of the elementals at the appropriate opportunity, and then appearing to you in time and place in beauty of blossom and succulence of fruit.

It is as if, through the devas, God is creating all the wonderful textures, shapes, scents, sounds, and tastes for all creation to enjoy and, through that enjoyment, be brought back to their source.

The physical being of our planet is manifested from many "inner" worlds, from "real" essences not necessarily tangible to our five senses. We have another sense that knows their reality: intuition, a sense of inner knowing. There is a sense in us, our divine discontent, that suggests that we notice and delve into whatever we feel is not right, and we go on until we find the only fulfillment, which is union with God.

As I see it, the seed quality of love births the unpolarized qualities that we call angelic and that we name by a positive aspect like joy, having no other words. These qualities themselves are the seeds for and give birth to the opposites: joy/sorrow. These in turn generate all the worlds, right down to the physical. I tried to trace what I considered a quality for the purpose of recognizing its expression on other levels. Courage, for example; how is it expressed or seen? On the emotional/ intellectual level there are lots of human symbols of courage: the power animal in shamanistic cultures, warrior gods like Mars, the lion in medieval times, the sign of Leo in astrology. All these are symbols of how we and nature express the sacred at times. In denser matter, what are the expressions of courage? The metal iron is the symbol of Mars, the color scarlet is the symbol of courage, and the sound of the drum brings courage in battle. According to Dr. Bach, who discovered flower essences to help us develop certain qualities, the flower essence of *mimulus* produces courage in us; in medieval times knights wore borage on their armor to maintain courage. There must be correlations everywhere, in chemistry, in physics. If certain qualities are outstanding in a personality, we may say that an individual is fit to be a leader or an artist, both vessels of power. When certain qualities are present in a mountain, we may recognize that mountain as a vessel of cosmic forces and call it sacred. At a chemical level, researchers are finding that qualities produce chemicals; for example, in a state of tranquillity the body makes *diazepam* (the main ingredient in Valium), in a state of exhilaration, it makes interleukin, in heightened emotion, adrenaline.

In our culture we are only beginning to see connections between qualities and matter. We recognize qualities expressed on the personality level as peace, joy, and so on. We recognize ourselves and others and even different cultures to be exhibiting certain qualities. We personally struggle with conflicting choices offered by differing ideals or emotions and are often confused by the dualities in ourselves. Our task is to bring the duality we perceive into wholeness again. In this bewildering modern life we have exempted our personalities from having divine attributes. We have many fears, but we do not know how to resolve or accept them, how to fit them into a spiritual life.

Personal Physical Connection

I myself was catapulted into taking a different approach on the physical level by a car accident early in 1992. I had no outward injuries, but I was shaken, resulting in a loss of strength in my arms and legs. I could just manage on my own, with the help of friends, and I tried various types of healing. Some months later a vivid dream seemed to indicate that as part of the healing process, it was time for me to resume a definite meditation schedule. I was glad; I had always felt rather guilty about having given up regular inner attunement, even though I knew it had been a fitting decision at the time, some twenty years earlier. So began another turn of the spiral. For me, meditation is a way of becoming increasingly aware of our divine natures. Now I drew the God part of me much nearer. I became more conscious of it as part of my personality and physical body during these periods. I certainly needed the sacred to be closer to my consciousness, for I have always had a poor self-image.

Previously I had completely ignored the physical part of me, for I had always been healthy. My body had never given me any trouble, and in return I had never given it any appreciation. Like most of us, I had to learn through suffering! I became aware of and for the first time sent love to that part of me responsible for my material body, that is, the intelligence of my physical holy temple. Holding it in my thoughts, I imagined the qualities of a healthy, functioning body. My physical elemental responded to the love; my guidance encouraged me to cease having thoughts of being separate from my body, emotions, and mind. For a time I focused on letting the Beloved be there in the personality and letting myself be there with the sacred, imagining it as part of my physical elemental. Poetically, I saw God as magic on the physical. A regenerated Dorothy. I also called on the Angel of Healing to join in. The meditative "appointments" were moving experiences and influenced me imperceptibly on the physical plane, just as my earlier attunements had gradually altered my consciousness. Other methods, like *jin shin*, an ancient Japanese technique for harmonizing the energy patterns and flows in the body, were part of the cure. Slowly my physical fitness improved. I began to appreciate the incredible wisdom that regulates the physical body. I wanted to cooperate with it—when I remembered! Tension on any level, of course, stresses the body.

During this time I also discovered a surprising interest in ritual. I have never been drawn to the outward symbols and ceremonials of past or present traditions; these seemed outmoded and impractical, even ludicrous, in the modern world. In fact, I have thoroughly disliked ritual, no doubt put off it by what seemed to me the spurious, canting voices and meaningless, repetitive actions of some Christian ministers in church, as well as by religious explanations that were not acceptable to me. But somehow life presented another face, and I found myself partaking in workshops given by people trained in the old Celtic tradition, experiencing journeys into their spiritual worlds, and finding value in certain symbolism. These events resulted in my assembling an altar in my apartment, something I had never previously needed nor found helpful. I now thought an altar would be a valuable reminder of what I wanted to remember at all times: the Beloved. On the altar I just put concrete symbols used in many traditions: earth, air, fire, and water (the four elements). I used hollowed stones for earth and water, a hurricane lamp with a candle for air and fire.

The Qualities of the Four Elements

This connection to ritual led to another type of attunement to the inner worlds and a deeper understanding of qualities and their manifestions. I connected inwardly to the four elements, which held a great silence, incredibly pure power, immense love. At first I rather shied away from such power, at least until my own level of love deepened. I had to go more profoundly into love than ever before; otherwise I felt the connection shallow and somewhat frightening. Strange, I thought, that I didn't have to go that deeply into love with God, the source and power of these elements. Then I realized that, of course, God, encompassing all levels of love, always meets us at our own level, always brings to us exactly what is right for us at the time. I certainly could not have attuned to those four elements years ago; it would have been too much. Now it was as if earth, air, fire, and water were the greatest of angels, the most ancient, the first formed, the first qualities, out of which everything is made. Indeed, in some traditions the first creation is the four elements. Anyway, I kept attuning to the elements and learning from them.

Previously the idea that life was divided into earth, air, fire, and water seemed silly to me, even though for centuries the doctrine of the four humors was accepted in medicine and philosophy. I had not realized that, in the Middle Ages, the explanation for natural phenomena was that all things were said to possess "essence," and that forms were incarnate ideas. Naturally I now took an interest in the four elements and looked for information about them. The medieval view, voiced by the Swiss-born physician and alchemist Paracelsus, was that these elements were active entities. According to him, they were essentially spiritual forces with a self-determining principle guiding their unfolding lives through time. Each element formed a world of its own, and each developed and evolved independently of the others through a consensus of actions. The elements did not mix in composition, but instead existed simultaneously and independently in each individual object. Predominant elements in the object determined the world to which it belonged and became its guiding soul.[1] In Greek philosophy, the elements are equated with the four human faculties: moral (fire); aesthetic and soul (water); intellectual (air); and physical (earth).[2]

Thinking more universally, I saw that in all creation these elements are present. They are primal powers, and we need to get down to basics. Today, in our dissatisfaction with life in the West, we are becoming aware of a loss of soul and a loss of quality. There is a new interest in the values of original cultures, in shamanism, where the power of the animals is sought. Power qualities in North American traditions are aspects of awareness, signs of a cosmic mind in natural forms. Our bodies have the intelligence to know that they are made of earth, air, fire, and water, at least when we return to nature, where many of us feel free and at home. The elements are wonderful icons for this age. They encompass the material and the spiritual. They are definite, physical examples for us to use in the working of spirit. The four elements seem appropriate to our materialistic age, canceling the notion that spirit is simply ethereal and insubstantial.

As creation proceeds, we humans continue to learn the sensitivities required for greater and more conscious life. The elements are working in us all in the deep silence of our beings,

---

1. Nicholson, Shirley, and Brenda Rosen, compilers. *Gaia's Hidden Life: The Unseen Intelligence of Nature*. Wheaton, Ill.: Quest Books, 1990.
2. Arroyo, Stephen. *Astrology, Psychology and the Four Elements: An Energy Approach to Astrology and Its Use in the Counseling Arts*. Davis, Calif.: CRCS Publications, 1975.

in a cosmic linking; the elements are the servants of quality in all worlds. The love I felt deepened. I increasingly realized how much the elements are part of us on the physical level, for our bodies include them all. But they do not live in just our bodies, though the four are the basic quality divisions necessary to create form; the four elements cover all dimensions. As they shared with me:

⌘

Of course we can speak as one, being one under Love. And we speak from the human dimensions as well as the cosmic, which you felt in our first contact, because we are in all dimensions. We first appeared as cosmic, since that is our true self, and should be seen as such. We are your servants and your masters, and it is best you know this. For too long, it seems to us, has man's ignorance ruled this planet, and yet we understand. It is well that you love paradox; nothing else can comprehend our identities! Although we "speak" in human terms, remember who we truly are, as well as being you. Yes, though God spoke to you in human terms, you could not at that time have received the vaster picture. Yes, you will love us; we will temper our strength to yours and help you understand the joy and creativity of the union of our four elements.

Although I have long been aware of the angels, the connection with the four elements helped me to have a deeper and more loving appreciation of the angelic world and of love itself. As the elements communicated:

⌘

We speak as one, and bow to Love. From it, and you, we sense longing and joy and such qualities, but these are not our possession in a human sense. We are more like machines, geared to do our jobs,

*and our great attribute is power, each in our own way. Of course,
we have intelligence and are well aware of our work. It is as if qualities are one dimension, and we are another, and we work together
and stay separate at the same time, which is difficult to understand
from a human point of view. In a sense we (qualities and elements)
feed each other; in another sense, we are the servants of sensitivity,
without having sensitivity ourselves and yet creating the environment and vehicles for it. There would not be consciousness as you
know it without us, and yet we are not conscious in the way you are.*

From this communication I had the idea that the elements
were insensitive, not compassionate: Did they feel the suffering
of those burnt in a fire, for example? They replied that they
did, and a thousand other feelings also, the causes and results
of life. How could they create something or someone with
greater awareness than themselves? They said that gradually I
would come to a better understanding and awareness of the
whole, that their love was vaster than we could comprehend. I
questioned, if love is the answer to all things, what of intelligence? For them, love is the basis of intelligence; without love,
there would be no reaching out, no questioning, no desire for
answers. Without love, intelligence can be just power, liable to
be separate, for even if it knows it is part of the whole, it is not
enough just to know. It is necessary to relate, which is what
love does. Looking back on this answer, it reminds me of the
cultural historian Thomas Berry's view that love is the alluring
activity of the cosmos, the primal dynamism.

Recently I had a personal experience of the relatedness of
love and intelligence. I experienced a great deal of worry and
anxiety about writing this book. The contents seemed to be a
mishmash of ideas, and my brain seemed to be a mush unable
to deal with them. I decided to do the Krishnamurti exercise,

to look at this aspect of myself that I thoroughly disliked without any judgment. I succeeded, and love came rushing in. To my surprise, not only did love fill me but my mind also functioned again. Intelligence was there with the love.

I also found that when I resonated more deeply with the elements, I received greater clarification. For them, whatever helps anyone reach subtler levels is to be promoted, whether or not the senses are used, whether we call on God, the Absolute, angels, qualities, elements. For me everything was part of the whole, and the elements said that the different foci present different attributes to be brought out, for there is an immense and mysterious spectrum in the universe, and each individual responds uniquely.

Through time I reached a closer connection with the elements, though always conscious of their deep, deep power as tools to grasp the highest realm. They stretched my understanding. For instance, they called the angels their friends, fellow workers, or playmates in the worlds, having sensitivity in many realms. Humans, they said, are created by both the elements and the angels, and we are capable of a great awareness. But we have a long way to go! We humans, having been given the gift of creativity, have to learn how to use tools. The elements are available at all levels for manifestation, and in learning to use them creatively, we learn to be aware of the positive and negative poles of their power, to understand both the danger and the exciting adventure of human life. I had to be very full of love to invoke the elements. Generally, I invoked the four as one. I also approached them individually, accepting the divinity in each. This attitude helped me appreciate the depth of each element in life: the grace and depth of the heaviness of earth, the joy of the freedom of air, the warmth of fire in my body, the mellowness and fluidity of water—and their opposites. From these experiences I was impressed by what a longing for love there must have been, must continue to be, for the unmanifest oneness to enable creation to come into existence, an existence making room for simplicity and complexity, for joy, pain, fun, and compassion! The myriad forms of life speak of these mysteries, and love is born anew. Love is always new, and there is immense room for it in every human heart. The world heart dreams on, as we humans choose.

The Elements in Everyday Life

I asked what use in everyday life is this new connection with the elements. The answer was that the greatest use is the power of love that resonates in me, in anyone, as we make the connection. It is that love from each of us that is needed in the world and that will change the environment. It is right to be focused on practical things, but it is the *attitude* with which practical things are done that betters any situation or relationship. This is so simple that it is constantly overlooked. Indeed, I had thought my love for God was as deep as possible, but it had to be deepened for the tremendous power of the elements. Many people at present feel uplift from the angels, and that is wonderful. The elements partake more fundamentally on all levels of life, including that of the angels, and therefore can be exceedingly useful and helpful for humankind. When I objected to the four elements as being an outdated medieval concept, I was asked to approach them as truth in the present, to see that they are a more potent part of life than any scientific theory and in fact are the basis of science.

If the elements are so strong on all levels, then their qualities act on what is purely physical and what is purely of the soul, and on all areas between. Everything in our world is created through the transformation of the elements; they are the active powers of the soul level of the world. On the physical and sensory levels, the function of the elements is fairly obvious: fire burns and transforms, water dissolves, and so forth. I tried to understand with greater depth the information on the elements given by many sources. A comprehensive and complete language of these energies is portrayed in the ancient science of astrology, where everything affecting humanity comes under one of these four divisions. The interaction of these forces, whether harmonious or challenging, is exquisitely laid out, although an understanding of the effects of the elements is naturally a matter of the extent of the individual's self-awareness. What meaning did the energies of the four elements convey?

Earth is the solid element, representing the physical world. It is a symbol for the creative power on the plane of matter, portraying material things like money and resources, work, tangible results, our normal conceptions of reality based on the senses, the concrete, rational mind. The land is a record of the past history of life. According to various schools of thought, we enter into a relationship with earth through contemplation.

Air is the gaseous element, a symbol for the creative power on the airy plane, the mind through which humanity becomes self-conscious. Air represents various aspects of the mind and of our human need to exchange information with others and with the environment. Through air qualities we can become detached and therefore sufficiently free of old patterns to call on the enormous potential of the creative mind. Air represents cosmic, dynamic movement. We relate to air through concentration.

Fire is the radiant element, a symbol for the creative power of spirit, energy, the initial source of life, representing the vital or etheric body. It relates to the function of intuition, the innate consciousness of individuality, and to our often limitless vitality, self-confidence, and enthusiasm evoked by intuitive perceptions. Fire symbolizes our sense of inner purpose or meaning, which we tend to call the urge for self-expression. Fire finds value in meaning and seeks meaning in all experiences. It is nonrational. It also represents cosmic, dynamic activity. We relate to fire through meditation.

Water is the liquid element, a symbol for the fluid emotional nature, for feelings, for the creative power of picture-making, that is, for the imagination, which reflects an inner sense of the outer world. Water represents the wish life, the feeling or astral body of humanity, and thus the world of causes for everything that happens to us in our external life. It also is nonrational. It signifies the power to absorb, to dissolve, and to recreate. We relate to water through empathy.

This is only a very brief and limited evaluation of the energies of the elements. By deepening our relationship to the initial qualities of each element, much understanding can be gained. The elements told me that when we see them as conveyors and administrators of the love that connects all things, we are more linked with all creation. The miracle of our existence can awaken love, and the elements can communicate with humans when they are acknowledged. When we consider the elements as part of God, we will link with them and act from wholeness instead of acting in a sense of separation from life. I worried that love would not be present when considering the elements, and they told me that the mind of humanity now needs a greater understanding of the universe, which they can provide. Even our current technology, such as computers, will not be understood fully until we acknowledge and love the elements. Of course, the mystery of life will not cease.

Other Symbols and Approaches to the Four Elements

I also became aware that the four elements are symbolized differently in other traditions. For example, the four directions (north, east, south, west), the four seasons (winter, spring, summer, autumn), the four worlds of the tree of life (expression, origination, creation, formation), the four evangelists (John, Luke, Mark, Matthew), and the sequence of stars, Sun, Moon, and Earth. I found that when I was summoning the qualities of an element in some situation, it was sometimes easier to use the symbols for the seasons, that "summer" would evoke in me a richer image of the qualities than "fire." Different images appeal to different people.

My interest in older traditions also connected me with magic—not magic produced by trick performers or magic as something supernatural or diabolic, but magic as a resonant, intuitive perception that predates modern physics and is in keeping with most modern theories of the relationship between matter and energy.[3] One day, with others, I took part in a ceremonial approach to other worlds during which I had to circle very, very slowly. I could not balance properly, because my legs were still recovering from my accident, and I suddenly called for help from the four elements. Immediately I was able to circle appropriately. Call that magic, which is also a name for the external working of energies we do not yet understand, (as television is magic to a primitive person), or call it the power of the elements. It worked. These elements are what everything is made of, projected through the creative power of love.

---

3. Stewart, R. J. *Living Magical Arts: Imagination and Magic for the 21st Century.* London: Blandford, 1987.

As I said earlier, myths present us with the archetypal sources for psychological events, which can move us to see things from a soul perspective. Within every archetype is a divine energy. Psychology holds that a divine archetypal figure can be contemplated only as a concrete image and that such imaging is not projection but creative imagination. I myself have not had a need for concrete images and have felt directly into quality, which has been my method of experiencing soul energies. For me, soul energies *are* qualities, and since we have all experienced various qualities, we can straightaway experience soul.

Another approach to soul energies is found in ancient Western traditions, which say that there are three states or worlds: the world of here and now, or physical reality, termed Middle Earth; the metaphysical world, or psychic (astral) reality, called the Otherworld; and the spiritual realm, which is the abode of the imageless Deity. According to Caitlin and John Matthews, authors of many books on Celtic and Arthurian traditions, these are crude distinctions that do not take into account the overlapping and interdependent nature of humanity, the ancestors, angels, and gods. In the past, Otherworldly concepts were bounded by the realm of ancestors, the Underworld. Shamans trained long years to make the journey to the ancestors, a journey fraught with danger. The Underworld was understood to have an entry that bordered Middle Earth, often a cave mouth.

The Otherworld went underground in Britain after the acceptance of Christianity and continued to flourish in secret. The church denied that Otherworldly beings, the Shining Ones, are real in their world. This is also true of the god forms of the native traditions, where the latent power of the elements was crystallized into gods. Otherworld beings range from the psychic equivalent of animals—the elementals—right up to the highly evolved spirits or energies that we know as gods, with a wide spectrum of variations that might be called angels or tutelary spirits.

Qualities from a Cosmological Viewpoint

In my continuing search for understanding, another piece of the puzzle was given me when I came across a treatise on cosmology by Vitvan, written in 1951, two years after I had attended his school. His erudite and complex teachings were difficult for me to understand, though I tremendously appreciated his pragmatic yet vast approach and learned much from him about how we react, how we blame others for our own actions, how we give value to words, and so on. Now his explanations seemed somewhat easier to understand. I was delighted to find him talking about qualities and the four elements in this paper.

Vitvan describes this world as an energy system. In any dynamic creative process, the first observable function is polarization, dichotomy, from an initial state of rest or neutrality. Through polarization, the negative force comes into function, that is, it becomes "space," or substance. The second action is that, from the same neutral state, positive power begins to act upon or in "space." The two poles form the axis for the lines of force, a web upon which a process emerges. A third action occurs simultaneously, in that a binding power, a controlling force, a balance, is located in the nonpolarized neutral state. The configuring light-energy substance locks together, resulting in a sphere of action for fire, air, water, and earth. Fire is the symbol for the dynamic essence of electricity or light; air the symbol for rarefied substance; water the symbol for the coalescence or consolidation of single units (electrons, protons, and neutrons) into energy systems called atoms, molecules, colloids, and so on. I can understand that concept somewhat by thinking of a hot or rarefied vapor for "air" condensing into liquid, "water." Earth is the symbol for the continuing condensation, or progressive cooling, of the energy systems into what we call things or objects, configurations of molecules, colloids, and crystalloid structures that we call form.

This process of polarization, the action of the positive force upon the negative substance, resulting in the spheres of action called fire, air, water, and earth, is a single continuous action labeled the "involutionary process." The three distinct actions are simultaneous, one action, resulting in the densest configuration and the laying down of a base for every possible aptitude, attribute, and quality that is potential in creation. These potentials are not manifest (*called Nirguna Brahma* in Hindu thought) but are brought out in the evolutionary process. We humans have every potential, every archetype, every possibility in our structure. This is another way of saying that all individuals function in an overall field, an Oversoul.

Vitvan explains this on the physical level using a cell as an example, for the cosmic process is repeated at all levels. Within the cell, in the process of mitosis a separation in the centrosome occurs, the positive and negative poles receding as far apart as the cytoplasm, or space, of the cell permits. The third action, which Vitvan says is in the realm of physics, is the influence of the neutron in the atom upon the negative electrons and positive protons. This third action is a binding power, a controlling force, a balance. According to Vitvan, the highest known Trinity is Positive, Negative, Balance. He emphasizes that the three actions are simultaneous functions, like lightning.

There are many precise, scientific descriptions in Vitvan's treatise on cosmology, including much about qualities, balance, rhythm. I was thrilled to find a concept putting into different words what I had discovered for myself, that from a central or neutral power, which I call God, come the qualities, symbolized by the four elements, from which all further creation proceeds. It is wonderful to have the feeling that the universe makes sense and that we, too, can participate in its development! Just as I was awed that the garden pea deva was in charge of all garden peas in the world, I was awed that the elements are in charge of everything.

Another Western view, described by Brian Swimme in *The Universe Is a Green Dragon*, I found wonderfully exciting. Swimme writes that "cosmic allurement" is the dynamic principle fusing the material plane, and that we humans experience that force as love. He writes of land (earth) as cosmic memory, frozen memory; of wind (air) as creative exuberance, movement; of fire as cosmic, dynamic, radiating energy; and of sea (water) as cosmic sensitivity, absorbing and becoming new. My description of these elements is much too brief, but the book is immensely mind opening.

My human mind can almost envision how qualities, guided by the innate intelligent love that is the source and life of everything, constructed worlds and forms. Just as I was helped and given sustenance in every area of my need during my times of attunement, though I didn't know what was being done, so all life has been helped to grow and become more conscious through the millenniums. Every need was met. There was a need for greater awareness, and, for example, sight was imagined. Eyes were brought into being, continually shaped and fashioned, evolved through the centuries in countless ways, to fit into current conditions. It is the same with all development. With infinite love and intelligence, worlds came into being and continue to change to meet prevailing requirements. Humans now have their part to play in the fashioning of our planet. While we have not been very successful because of our limited visions, we are learning. The intelligent love within us continues to guide us all the way, and we can choose to cooperate consciously by "listening" to it.

Opening to Quality

Opening ourselves to what we truly are, deepening the qualities that we as humans encompass, and living from a loving center mean that we become fully human, fully divine. Yet to be conscious of our spiritual selves is not an easy matter, though it is our human task. In my workshop attunement sessions, as I have mentioned, we aimed to claim that spiritual self, by returning to a peak experience through memory and imagination. From that clear space we focused on resonating with a certain quality. It is difficult to make a blank mirror of our minds in order to become one with the quality and then receive pure inspiration, for we are not educated in the art of "listening." It had taken me years of practice to be open to newness, to extend my boundaries into unknown dimensions, to perceive love in all its aspects, to see things as qualities rather than quantities, to see "things" as "activities." When we name things, make nouns of them, we settle them into a static form, repressing the livingness in them. This is such an integral part of our culture that we take it utterly for granted. Paintings often open us to seeing that things can speak to us, but on the whole we deal with objects as dead. In our everyday living, we can stop identifying ourselves as stuck within our emotions by saying "Fear is present" instead of "I am afraid."

With love, we link up with life everywhere. With love, we communicate and speak with life on all sorts of levels, for all life comes from the seed qualities, which, in turn, are inherent in love. As we take a step and put forth an ounce of effort, we will be met and encouraged in a multitude of ways.

Exercise:

1. Choose some quality or attribute that you find helpful, or would like to experience, for example courage. Attune to the highest state that you know, as suggested previously, and in that state become your chosen quality, become courage. If thinking of some image of courage helps bring the quality more vividly to life for you, think of the god Mars or Popeye or Superman, or whatever suits you. The aim is not to think of examples of people being courageous, but instead to summon the energy and become it. Resonate with that quality in yourself, bring it out into your awareness. By accepting and becoming familiar with your chosen quality in the exercise, it is easier to invoke it at other times in everyday life. People have found that this exercise has helped them considerably in dealing with situations that give them an opportunity to use the quality.

2. When in some situation in your life you immediately need a certain quality, ask for it, ask for help. Invoke any relevant image, like the elements or Jesus.

⌘ Part 2

⌘ CHAPTER FOUR

SOULS OF NATURE

AT PRESENT, although there is a growing appreciation of the values of cultures that live close to the land and to nature, on the whole we live without multidimensional links to minerals, plants, and animals. Yet these links are always there, and often simply being in nature brings relaxation and peace. Something innate in us is happy in nature, quite apart from what we learn from it.

As well as living ecologically and working for the welfare of the planet, we can consciously connect and cooperate with the intelligence of nature through meditation, through love. Minerals, plants, and animals have group souls. For instance, the soul aspects of a marigold and of a wisteria are unique and have different qualities, different angels. These angels, these souls, are in charge of all life of a particular species, though divisions are not as rigid as we believe from our material viewpoints. Some of our animal pets, however, are developing individuality in varying degrees. Each human is unique and individualized, having its own soul level, its own angelic energy. With love we enter the soul level of all other worlds, consciously or unconsciously. With love we discover the love inherent in all life.

Trees

When I first contacted the soul essence of trees, the vital need for large trees on the surface of the Earth was communicated to me. The same message was repeated again and again wherever and whenever I attuned to, or "listened" to, the trees. The urgency and emphasis on this one aspect of nature made an impact on me, for this very first message from the tree angels was compelling and weighty. It felt so different from the gentle, loving help I received from all other angelic intelligence. I thought I might be psychotic or quite wrong, because at the time, in the early sixties, I had not encountered the opinion that cutting trees was endangering something and I felt very much alone. Gradually these views received confirmation from sources I trusted, the first being from the British forester Richard St. Barbe Baker, who had founded the organization Men of the Trees and had worked all his life to conserve them. My paranoia on the subject ceased, and I eased my conscience by mentioning the need for large trees on the surface of the Earth whenever I gave a public talk. Although linking with the plant aspect of nature has not been my main concern for several years, still the message of the large trees remains valid and critical.

Trees absorb and breathe out water, bind the soil, change water levels below the earth, alter the chemical elements in the air, and affect temperature, climate, and weather. On these physical levels we know how the four elements affect trees. Dynamic interchange with the soul level exists in all of life on the physical level. We see these interchanges manifested in the myriad interrelationships of nature. Tree felling is the cause of many so-called natural disasters, like floods and drought. Destroying trees, the respiratory organs of the planet, can create a greenhouse effect. We know that the rain forests harbor a vast selection of plant and animal genes, and we are beginning to realize that this wonderful reservoir can be used in many ways to help humanity, especially medically.

Even on mental and emotional levels, trees have a huge impact. The nature of their being brings steadiness, peace, and a thousand lessons on the interconnectedness of life. The quality of our thinking and of our feeling is harmonized by trees. They have their own aura, their own sound and scent. All these things affect us, and the lack of them, especially in the clattering, metallic din of a city, can disturb even the sanity of humans. A benign environment is usually necessary for us to develop and use our higher sensitivities, and a modern city offers little aid or comfort to people. When I am upset, I can regain peace and clarity by leaning against a tree or going for a walk among trees, especially evergreens like pines. Trees offer their balancing solace to us. One tree angel suggested that all large cities should have an adjoining forest for this very purpose.

Our shortsighted views have led to such a ravaged condition on Earth that they cannot continue to be applied without fatal results to ourselves and the planet. We have also been led to realize that our Western ideas of "wholeness," our ideas of God, have not included nature, though primal peoples instinctively do not have this limitation and consequently revere all life. Still, thinking people, even governments, recognize some of the values of trees and the implications of removing them. Our unecological treatment of the planet has made such vast changes that we have been forced to notice the danger of deforestation throughout the world. Yet trees, at the time of this writing, are still being slashed and burned at the rate of two acres per second.

The perspective that I have received from tree intelligence emphasizes other factors, such as the vital importance of the special energies channeled by mature trees as opposed to immature trees. Such a perspective may not be widely accepted, yet it may contain clues to unexplored areas for research. But the underlying truth, that trees are needed, is the same.

Acting on information regarding the need for trees, however, entails vast changes in our viewpoints and in the organization of our society, both economically and socially, and so far we have more or less continued with our old values. Thousands of people all over the world are fighting for the trees, and pro-tree lip service is even paid by government and lumber companies. But tree felling continues and even escalates as business hurries to gain wood for profit before any laws stop them. People rightly fear that they will lose their livelihood—and fear is a slave driver. Frankly, the cost is so great that we have preferred to make only cosmetic changes. We have continued to treat the wealth of the Earth, whether it be trees, minerals, or the land itself, as if it were there for our indiscriminate use, as if we have the inalienable right to do what we wish with it.

Only recently has it occurred to us that the disappearance of a species that took millions of years to develop might have an adverse effect on our own lives, that species other than human might have their own rights, and that at present the human species is the most dangerous and destructive one on Earth. We in the West have taken for granted that we have been given dominion over the Earth. Acting like lords, we have ignored the responsibilities of lordship. Accidents such as the nuclear crisis at Chernobyl, the chemical release at Bhopal, and the oil spill from the Exxon Valdez, are opening our eyes. But it is not easy to give up our comfortable habits and life-styles, or to stop supporting business by our prodigal use of cars, by our eating hamburgers provided by cattle raised in felled tropical forests or inhumanely killed, by our waste of miles of newsprint for our newspapers and junk mail, by our putting our money into armaments—the list in our wasteful society goes on and on.

Do the tree species themselves have any opinions about our actions, and is their work affected? Always I find that perspectives from the soul level, whether of trees, humans, or any other sphere, are very different from those of our limited rational minds. Their view is from the millenniums, and they see us rather like teenagers learning to behave from mistakes and experiences as we grow. They also see our magnificent potential and make allowances for our behavior.

I experienced one example of their vast perspective in 1974 in the Avenue of the Giants in California, where redwood trees are being preserved. I delightedly stepped into a grove to enjoy these giant trees that were being preserved, as a sign there said, "in perpetuity." While looking at the trees, I noticed that the tops were dying. And these were the very ones, the only ones, protected from being cut. I was sick at heart. "Why?" I wondered. Perhaps because we've dammed the rivers that fed alluvial mud to the trees. Perhaps because we've poisoned the air with car exhaust, or because we've compacted the ground as we walked around them. Whatever the reason, I wept. Then I decided to ask the soul of the redwood tree species itself, and received this message:

⌘

Small mortal and great being, we greet you. Come with us up high above the traffic noise and human pettiness to where everlasting peace is. Let the "evil" be as dust on your feet, to be shaken off and turned to the peace of God, the creative peace that cloaks a planet and many forms of life. What if the trees come toppling down? Our vibrations are forever part of life here, and we are glad to have contributed as much as we have. We rejoice, for life moves on. Whatever form it takes, it is one life, as we well know. We are part of you; you are part of us. And so it will always be.

My immediate reaction to this response was a much stronger inward determination to see that the wonderfully majestic form of life we call redwood should not perish from the planet. I realized that our human choices regulate much of the fate of species on Earth, and it was my definite choice that redwood trees remain. But for a long time I have not shared this particular message, since I believed that it could be interpreted as meaning it was all right to cut trees down instead of emphasizing the opposite effect it had on me, an effect that wise tree angel probably anticipated. I now believe that sharing it can help expand our views of life.

As we use more wilderness areas and as more and more species become extinct, I have realized that many nature energies are being withdrawn. This is not happening through the natural processes of evolution but through our shortsighted, immediate human choices. What has taken millions of years to develop suddenly no longer exists and is irretrievably lost. The incredible diversity and richness of life on the planet lessens each day and will continue to do so as long as we treat the planet with our present ignorance, irreverence, greed, and selfishness.

As a North American who has experienced the joys of true wilderness and has felt the incredible wonder of it, the harmony and peace of it, I should hate to have untouched wilderness disappear from the Earth. Of course, wilderness has almost vanished already, but national parks do still offer areas of nature that can bring healing to the human heart and soul. There is beauty everywhere in nature, in deserts or bogs or ice, but a forest offers such special amenities, such unique solace and peace and clarity, that I hope all future generations can share that joy. We would be much poorer without large trees, and it would be my human choice to preserve wilderness areas.

Can the trees still do their work, now that they are so few?

Not as well. I have flown over areas of the East coast of North America where almost all old-growth trees had been removed and where young trees have rooted in the farms deserted as pioneers moved west to cultivate more land. I found that the overlighting forces were like nursemaids, patiently waiting for their charges to grow up and become mature enough to begin their functions. All over the planet trees are being felled, and this practice is causing great transformation. There are not sufficient trees to transmit the energies necessary for their purpose in planetary life. They tell me that, as always, the energies are changing, and even that some of these energies are for humans to transmit. What these "energies" are specifically I don't know, although I do know that they are qualities of love.

Since the urgency regarding trees came to me many years ago, I wondered more recently what the view of the tree angels is now. I received this message:

⌘

The subject is as urgent as ever. Humanity has begun to realize the necessity for trees on the surface of the planet, and we rejoice that this is so. Until now you have been learning to change your actions through the results they bring, through the suffering you have undergone, and this will continue until you truly change and cease cosmetic measures. As a planetary species, you have developed your minds and hearts sufficiently to enable you to change without suffering, to consciously choose to follow inner knowing—which is now confirmed through the farsightedness of your minds and the loving feelings of your hearts. You can change, and deal with the consequences you fear in a helpful way, and the trees give you a wonderful opportunity to practice now. There is nothing you cannot overcome with dedicated minds and hearts, and you have the angelic world with you as you come into your greater abilities.

The trouble is, I wish I always had the patience and the cosmic views of the angels! It is so obvious to me that we have to modify our behavior, have to deal with our worlds in different ways, and that those changes come first within ourselves. But this is not evident to many people.

Naturally, we can support the forests in any way that seems right to us: planting trees, supporting environmental groups, not buying newspapers, and the like. When we feel or see no separation of trees, the planet, and ourselves, we close a gap. We can be outward tree missionaries, or we can be most influential in the powerful thought and feeling world. It is the limited, separatist views of life that have brought about the present chaos, yet any of us can change. We can look at the nature world and marvel; it *is* marvelous. The more we look, the more we notice. And we can be grateful for it. As we consciously link up all areas of ourselves, letting the soul, the mind, the emotions, and the body be equal partners in this great adventure of life, we constructively change everything we come across. And any expression of love for the whole from anyone helps build our knowingness that we are part of the Earth. The stronger that expression, the more powerful the results.

A deeper cooperation with nature is indeed needed. This may be achieved by a constant outward study of nature's intricacies, but in my experience that cooperation is also possible in our rich inner selves. Many people feel a link with nature, and many long for deeper links, but at present many more are likely to continue on their way without considering nature as anything like an equal partner. We need to develop the soul link. Then, as humans acting with the love that is ours to develop and express on Earth, we can co-create with nature.

Once I came across a special partnership with nature in a garden. To me, even the most well-planned, well-cared-for, and lavish gardens do not offer the same vitality, harmony, richness, freedom, and wholeness as any wild area does. I had even given up expecting that any garden would. I kept remembering contacting the essence of a little wild violet peeping out from sand dunes and finding that its power was greater than that of any carefully nurtured garden rose. But one day, as I walked along a street in suburban Amsterdam, I noticed a small garden where I felt the same vibrant energy as in the wilderness. I realized that a higher type of collaboration between humans and nature is actually possible after all. Outwardly that garden did not seem unique, and I could not spot what the difference was. Or perhaps I was too excited to notice. Maybe I was given the experience to open my mind to the wonderful possibilities of a human-made garden with the uplifting qualities of wild areas. It seemed to me that the owners of this garden must have had a conscious caring, sharing, love, and gratitude in creating it. Naturally it contained trees! For me, it was a prototype for co-creation with life.

Another new experience was when I found that nature and the people on a plain in one part of China were truly joined, for instead of two overlighting angels, one of humanity and one of nature, there was only one. No doubt this was because the area had been cultivated for thousands of years. The people's feel for nature was creative and loving, and might be a precursor of what could happen in other places in the world as we realize that our separation from nature is an illusion.

By aligning all parts of ourselves—our physical body, emotions, mind, and soul—our knowing area, our intuition, can guide our actions. In my opinion, this is what human development is all about: committing all of ourselves to the greater whole of which we are a part. We can "listen" within and without and find that we are part of that whole. More specifically, any of us can recognize, or have faith in, the existence of the higher forces of nature—that is, the soul of nature, the angelic world (our own soul nature included)—and thereby open the door to awareness of life in a different and more personal way. Intelligent nature forces welcome communication from us. We meet the world of nature in ourselves, the microcosm, and find a personal and meaningful relationship as we experience this intelligence, bringing change to the planet. Just a recognition, a belief, makes for the needed openness.

We are not limited to following our ingrained cultural biases and the shortcomings of our education. When we explore ourselves, we find that we are one with the universe. Then all our actions can stem from that part of ourselves that includes the planet and therefore the forests. When we in the West enthroned reason, in the necessary development of our intellect, we cut off or controlled our instinctive knowing. Now that our environment is forcing us to see our shortsightedness and to realize that all life is linked, we can begin to open up to a higher spiral of ourselves, an intuitive understanding that includes, but is not limited to, instinct. We can bring wisdom into all areas of life. We can appreciate that in a natural forest or desert it is easier to have a living experience of God, for these areas are temples capable of taking us beyond our ego and transforming us.

Volcanoes

Of course, the love and intelligence that I call God is in everything, and to me it is particularly wonderfully and beautifully expressed in nature. Yet we talk of the fury of Mother Nature, of her vengeful power or of the violence of wind or sea as acts of God. We have made nature our scapegoat in many areas. I had a great example of the lack of validity of this view when I had an unprecedented opportunity to contact an active volcano. Mount St. Helens, which I had visited some years previously, started rumbling. I found that, seen from the soul level, the mountain was doing an intricate, complicated, intense dance in an effort to balance all the forces. It communicated this message:

⌘

These are adjustments that must be made. Volcanic mountains are always linked and aware of the larger picture below the surface of the Earth, which, in turn, is affected by the larger picture above the surface of the Earth. Although we do not make the calculations and decisions, we are akin to them, linked, one in intent, and a vehicle for plans and decisions. It is a delicate task, given the explosive tendencies of fire, especially at these times, when humankind has made those tendencies more volatile on the planet. We believe there will be a larger eruption here and seek our ingenuity to blend all forces to a fine, polished result.

Volcanoes seem powerfully uncompassionate to you humans, but this is not so. The strength of the fire element is everywhere needed, in your bodies, in your smelters, in the Earth, in the Sun. Recognize that power in yourselves and dedicate it to the whole; be as accurately precise in the gift of your lives.

While marveling at the complexity of the dance, I said nothing about an eruption. I thought I might be projecting that result from mere rumblings, when no one else was doing so, as far as I knew. But a short time later Mount St. Helens did explode.

Hurricanes

Twelve years later I had a similar experience with Hurricane Andrew:

⌘

I am an obliterator of extremes, blending hots and colds, dryness and wetness, before these extremes get too far apart. This must be done, for the maintenance of the planet's balance. If humans and their works are affected, still this must be done, for the whole.

You question if humans are part of the causes. Yes, they can be, and, yes, they can influence the process. As greater love and balance is attained in human attitudes, there could be fewer extremes. Nevertheless, remember that extremes are necessary to bring about knowledge, experience, and balance.

So, as in many other areas, I realized that the principle of balancing applies in all aspects of nature.

Minerals

I began my contact with the soul essence of nature with the vegetable world, and at first had no contact with the mineral-world essence. After some years, one day when I was admiring a pretty beach pebble, I wondered if there was an angel connected with it. I decided to try to attune to it. Here my cultural background immediately became evident, for I expected an undeveloped angel, because in our classifications minerals are less developed than plants. I expected a sort of monkey angel, but when I went to the soul level I found myself in the vastest presence, apart from God, that I had yet encountered, one that seemed to stretch into eternity. I called it the Cosmic Angel of Stone and received this powerful message:

⌘

Yes, I whom you have contacted am concerned with vastly more than your planet, for I contain or am connected with mineral life that exists in various stages throughout creation. Nature is full of paradox, in that as you seek contact with what you consider a lower form of life, you in fact contact a more universal being. The human mind codifies and formulates, which is within its right and purpose, but forgets that all is one, that God is in all, and that the basic substance of life, which seems most devoid of sensitive consciousness, is held in its state of existence by its opposite, a vast consciousness, too vast for you to do more than sense its fringes and know that it extends beyond your imagination as yet. You realize, too, that dense matter is influenced in its makeup by stellar energies.

It was the beauty of this particular stone that drew you to me. Beauty is of God, beauty is working out in all levels of life. Consciousness of beauty brings you into oneness, into any part of the universe. You are contained in it just as I seem to contain universes within myself. The more you appreciate beauty, the more you are linked universally. It is good to seek the life of it at high levels, for then your consciousness is expanded.

You feel right now that you can only look at every pebble with deepest reverence and worship, because you know it is part of my vastness. We are glad that in this way you have been shown a very little of the glory of God. The glory of God is everywhere, stretching from the farthest reaches of the universes to the little grain of sand, one and the same thing, held in eternal love and timeless with life.

Yes, of course it would be good to tune into me if you work with stone. Reverence all life, emulate my patience, unfold the mysteries of God and even of pebbles. Do it as a learner of life, a revealer. Let your dominion be over yourself and let your expanding consciousness see God's life in all things, where indeed it is—and, as you have learned, in the most surprising things. The color and sparkle of a stone is wonderful, but more wonderful is the consciousness that has brought about and continues to bring about these outer manifestations and grows cosmically. We are all part of the one life, no higher or lower. Praise God forever in the vastness of all life.

This experience completely reversed my evaluation of rocks and metals, and my new understanding found confirmation in a work by Rudolf Steiner saying that only an intelligence closest to the Godhead would be willing to incarnate in such a rigid form as the mineral.

An incident at Findhorn offered me another opportunity for expanding my views. One day I went shopping in nearby Elgin and returned to find that the community had borrowed a bulldozer to clear an area of grass and gorse for a building. I felt miserable at the sight of the devastated patch and knew something was wrong. On that day our contact with the elemental kingdom, Ogilive Crombie, phoned from Edinburgh to ask what was going on, for the nature spirits had come to him in anger and threatened to leave the garden. I sought clarification from the Landscape Angel. It inquired whether we had warned the plants of the impending bulldozing. We had previously learned that when one explained to weeds, for example, one's intentions to clear them out and gave the reasons, the energy of the plants would be withdrawn and the plants would be very easy to pull from the ground. The Landscape Angel wondered if we realized that there were etheric life forms whose homes in the surface of the land we had destroyed. It also asked if the driver of the bulldozer, a group member, had attuned to the machine in love. The answer to these three questions was no. The driver, who was also a motorcycle enthusiast, said that he wished we had requested him to attune, because he often became one with his machines. Our apologies to the nature spirits were accepted, and we learned some valuable lessons.

The mineral aspect of the planet is probably given less consideration by humans than any other part. Metals seem to just be dead life, and it is difficult to think of them otherwise. We extract them from the earth, we fire them, mix them, disintegrate them, compress them, pressure them, explode them, shape them, purify them, manufacture them, and so on. Our modern technological wonders are forged from them. Yet we take metals completely for granted; it wouldn't occur to us to thank them. They are merely dirt, inert substance. Yet they too are divine life. Only recently, now that we have polluted our soil and so loosened it by tree felling or ploughing that it washes away into rivers and oceans, have we begun to realize its essential value for our own life.

I came across a refreshing approach to the mineral world some years ago. In San Francisco people were being taken on nature walks, nature in this case being the stones of the skyscrapers. On such outings, the leader, who had studied the history of each building, the source and story of the marble or granite, related all this information to us. As we listened, we noticed and appreciated the character and polish of the stones. It even seemed that the rocks themselves were pleased to have been taken out of the dark earth, burnished, and placed to gleam in the sun. On another occasion I remembered attuning to a rock that had been taken from its original setting and used as an altar piece. How grateful it was to have been appreciated and brought there! In return, it was giving stable and strong rock energies to the area.

Through the years I have had intermittent links with the mineral world, particularly with crystals, since they have such pure, recognizable, and colorful forms, and seem to be the flower of the mineral kingdom. Two that seemed to be available more often than not, because I or someone else often had samples with us, were quartz crystals and amethysts. The quartz crystal always radiated mental clarity, precision, focus, and, often, a sense of gratitude toward us for freeing it to do its job, even a sense of fulfillment. The amethyst once greeted me with a rippling loving joy, because it was unusual for humans to come to it without desire and greed. It was a great, peaceful lover of beauty. I once sensed that a new angel was taking charge of it for some reason unknown to me, the only time I have experienced a shifting of responsibility.

Limestone essence seemed to have nerve lines connecting all over the Earth and carried the sense of a tremendous, changing past, although rather remote from humanity. I had the impression that we have much to learn from limestone. Opal essence gave a lovely, swirling, feminine feeling, a happy energy that was working to refine the sensibilities. I realized that minerals do, indeed, influence people and the land.

We need to incorporate in our thoughts more of the recognition of and reverence for Mother Earth's mineral life, in addition to plant and animal life, that is prevalent in primal peoples. Such honor is not only necessary for our survival but can also be a joy. It links us with our world. With it we regain a sense of belonging and are touched in deep areas of ourselves. We are part of the Earth; we need to protect it and love it and also enjoy it. After all, we are the Earth's consciousness moving on to greater awareness.

If we love enough, we experience the marvelous and delicate network of life. Through love we recognize the soul qualities in nonthinking Earth forms. The scope of Earth consciousness extends far beyond our physical ecological balance. There is the dancing joy of soul life, which we see expressed in the amazing physical forms of all categories of nature when we are free enough to be open to its beauty and to love. These brief expressions are, I hope, illustrations of some of the infinite dynamics of Earth life.

Animals

In early societies animals and plants were human beings' teachers, the gods of the time, and most tribes took on animal protectors. North American Indians generally think that animals, because the fundamental life force appears naturally in them, can be helpful powers to humans. Animals generally have group souls, but some of our pets who have close contact with humans begin to develop individuality and can be contacted on the personality level. Because animals are developing emotions, we emotional humans experience a closer connection with them than with minerals or plants, which function without emotions.

I made an early inner contact with the group soul of cats when I inquired about the recurring problem of well-fed domestic cats killing birds and mice. I was told to ask myself if humans are dependable enough to be responsible for feeding the cat world. I then remembered that when we had arrived in the Findhorn trailer park, which is adjacent to a Royal Air Force base, it was overrun by wild, diseased, and starving stray cats. These pets had been deserted when their owners, R.A.F. personnel, were posted to other areas. We had tried to help the cats, but were so unsuccessful that we had to call in the humane society. I realized that we humans are not dependable in our animal stewardship and that it is necessary for cats to keep their instincts intact. Our own fat pet cat, Susie, had proved that she understood very well when I talked to her. I had asked her in plain English to be at a certain place at a certain time, and, to my surprise, she was indeed there at the appointed hour. But whenever I mentioned she should not catch birds, mice, or voles and said that we would feed her, it was as if she drew a blind down and became utterly deaf; she couldn't understand at all.

Now and then it has seemed right to contact animal energies. One such time was when I came across brown bears in Alaska. The bear soul was almost crying with joy at the contact, because it was not used to having love focused on it. It had this to say:

⌘

On the soul level, in our mission as part of the planet, we are one. In our separation we are separate, and in that separate state terrible things happen. We have to be what we are, to be our bearness and defend ourselves when we must. So remember we are bear. Still we love you, and when you walk in love, we know. When you walk in love you are walking with your destiny, and nothing will harm you that your destiny does not bring you. When you walk in love you help all creation, and you fulfil our destiny, too. So please walk in love. It means so much to life. We look forward to the time when we can enjoy each other.

I don't know why the brown bear had such a philosophical message, but it helped me respect its uniqueness and the different paths that we each travel.

I had an interesting interchange with a raven at the rim of the Grand Canyon. It hopped by, and I had a feeling of its deep-throated joy, of its freewheeling, of its recognition of humans, of an endless searching (for food?), of the process of life, of love of the wind. For some reason, I asked it the question I was pondering at the moment: "How does one get closer to God?" It replied: "By flying!" I realized what a true answer that was. When one moves closer to God, one leaves the old world of thought and feeling and experience, and soars into new dimensions, a true flight. Then the raven flew past me, a couple of feet away, almost touching the ground on either side of me and making a noise unlike a caw. Later I discovered that my friend Ron, who shared giving workshops with me and who was down in the Grand Canyon while I was staying on the rim, had seen a raven fly very near him, upside down and looking right at him, at the same time as my encounter. We both felt very blessed by raven energy.

During the workshops Ron and I gave we usually attuned to animals, very often to the dogs that were around. These experiences were always interesting, always different, always permeated with love. I remember one dog so tied in consciousness to her owner that, even if sleeping, she could sense when the owner wanted her and would immediately awake and respond.

In 1987 I spent some weeks on an island off northern Vancouver Island with a group trying to communicate with orcas by broadcasting music underwater. In my type of communication I was first aware of orca energy as very light and playful, aware of our group attempts. The orca to me is a wonderful mixture of complexity and simplicity. It is aware on many different levels, very intelligent, and seems to joyfully accept life as it is. It seemed to indicate to me in that communication that long ago when mammals returned to water, they chose a path of individuation more linked with the whole than that of humans, more aware of others on physical levels. For instance, when they journey each day in search of food and in love of movement, there is a consciousness linking with whatever they pass, a recognition and blessing in a lighthearted way. Perhaps all animals are more a part of their environment than we humans are, but the cetaceans know it.

During another attunement with the orcas, I clearly linked with and experienced an understanding of the whales' soul level, with its usual feelings of love and joy. I also had contact on the personality level, for the orca has a complex mind that functions differently from the human mind. Its thought pattern is unlike ours. I had much difficulty understanding it and had to become accustomed to it through continued contacts before I could make any sense of it. I had to be very childlike and patient. Finally I thought I came to understand their mental patterns. This experience helped me realize that, like humans and unlike more primitive nature forms, such as trees, orcas have personality patterns, though they have a greater group feeling than we have.

On a later occasion, when I was aware of their angelic level, the orcas spoke as a group, expressing qualities that I had to put into my own human understanding, as follows.

⌘

Yes, we would like to have contact with you. You are as strange to us as we are to you, with all your repressions. We are freer in expression, more joyful, and, like you, have our limits and misuse our powers. Our joy is sometimes carried too far: it is both our strength and our weakness. Yes, we function in groups.

It seems that when I opened my mind in communication, the orcas gained, at least temporarily, my human understanding and realized that we function more as individuals. I feel that this is true of other angelic communication. When we contact other life, we open up to them a bridge to help them understand us better.

⌘

Yes, we are more aware and at one with the forces of the environment, more like your primal peoples. We have more energy, lots of curiosity; we are sort of open-mouthed with life. We think in waves of energy, not deliberation of the past.

On another occasion the orca's consciousness gave me some thoughtful advice in their own way:

⌘

Why don't humans relax more? Have fun? In love we can play together, and any past errors in the human/orca relationship can be dissolved. We don't need to cling to the past; the present is what is now. You don't need to feel guilty, not with love.

Later I had the opportunity to link with a related family of mammals, the spinner dolphins in Kealakekua Bay off the island of Hawaii. While my friends were swimming with these dolphins, I remained ashore and found that inner attunement came very easily. Perhaps it came easily because many humans had already made a pathway in such communication and the dolphins themselves did not find it unusual, as most animals did in my experience. The dolphins conveyed that they had difficulty in understanding our human sense of fear. Fear to them is a friend that helps them navigate. Our strong human desire to be with them they found strange, since they function in the present moment.

⌘

We just are. We are trying to understand you just as you are trying to understand us. When you are loving there is no problem. Your anticipation also is something for us to wonder at; it does not exist in the same way with us.

They went on to say that they realized the world is in a time of change, when humans are making a deeper connection with all life, in which they are active partners. They are trying to do their part in this change by helping prove to humankind the intelligence and love of other species. They themselves are, like the Alaskan bear, what they are. The dolphins seemed interested in my formulations and in picking up our knowingness, which helps toward greater planetary understanding.

At another locale, a Gila woodpecker felt no need to communicate with humans, since it fitted into its environment very precisely and smoothly. When I asked if there was any obstruction between it and humans, it replied no, not necessarily, that was just the way things were. It suggested the need for mystery!

I believe that at some time emotions began to develop in the animal world. We see that with our pets, and we have a deep heart response to their presence, as they certainly do to ours. I was reminded of this once when contacting a deer; I remember attuning to the animal first on the personality level, but it was not available to me. So I turned to the angelic level and made immediate contact. Then the emotional level was relayed to me, conveying a sense of great liquid eyes and gentleness, a reaching out to humans in an almost pleading way. This incident helped me recognize that I preferred contact with the completely free and unburdened higher levels, my usual pattern. However, while at the emotional level, I accepted and loved the energies of innocence there, with the knowledge that hurt can enter.

Upon relating to a frog, I was aware of strong energy almost exploding out in dark personality lines, while the devic level was like white light in the same shape. I tried to attune to a brain and was met with a rather baleful froggy eye. A Nepalese butterfly had a very peaceful angelic counterpart as well as scattered, unfocused areas. It said that although my contact with the plant world was very peaceful, with it I was encountering the beginning consciousness of insects. A buffalo nearby expressed a similar mixture of higher and lower levels—an energetic sense of service and intelligent knowingness in helping humans, along with a giving, milky, slow-moving laxness of a serving kind. A vulture berated me for judging the work of vultures, saying it does a job that needs doing, however awkward that seems to us.

It was a rhinoceros in Nepal that most confounded my conservationist self. I sensed from this animal a tremendous sweetness, seemingly so unlike its clumsy, armored body, and it communicated this:

⌘

The sweetness is a balance for the energies I must use in my physical form. I am glad you have found it and recognized the essence; keep it in mind. Yes, I remember your loving my African cousin. No, I am not worried that I might become extinct; it might be better to have a form in which the sweetness can be expressed more clearly. Thank you for your love, and accept ours.

It was wonderful to find from this ancient animal a freedom from attachment to form. It reminded me again of the constant plea from the angelic world for me to accept that life is change. Yet I had many reservations about sharing this rhinoceros message, because I feared that people would take it as an excuse for continuing practices that bring extinction to species and thereby lose the richness contained in myriad life forms.

From Brazilian monkeys I had impressions of what is learned as a monkey, a sense of rich growth. Under soul guidance, there was development of curiosity and intelligence. I also gained a strong idea of the ceaseless love that radiates from the soul level toward animals. The monkey oversoul was glad to receive the love of our small group of people as we attuned to the wild monkeys. There was a feeling that generally they were more used than loved. Of course, this feeling of their being used could very well have been a projection of mine. Our understanding is always colored by our mind-sets. I know that some of my early messages from the plant world were somewhat marred by my belief that humans were thoughtless and selfish in dealing with forests in particular, which resulted in my ascribing my own anger to nature. Later I realized there was no anger at the soul level, in the angelic world, and that it is by the visible results of our thoughtlessness and selfishness that we humans learn.

I had an experience that made me wonder if the unseen energies of a country, related as they are to human power, influence animal behavior and the natural environment. In Katmandu, for instance, the dogs work and respond as a group. In different parts of the city there are dog guardians, with a lead dog, which protect the village area. Nightly there is the most wonderful chorus of barking, baying, droning, whining, all sounded together. Then comes a silence, and when for some reason the lead dog barks again, the canine symphony resumes There is no individual barking. However, in a Western city, in Brazil, I became aware of a difference in dogdom; there was also much barking at night, but it was of individual dogs, not a group. Perhaps dogs can partake either of group or individual development, for generally in the East group participation is primary and in the West individual development. Everywhere such creatures as frogs act in unison, but that may be because most animals are not as open to human influence as dogs. Animals open our hearts, and, indeed, dogs are being used as therapy for healing loneliness among older people. With love at the soul level, our connections grow even closer, and we can consciously cooperate with animals in a new and wonderful way.

It is heartening to encounter increasingly greater numbers of individuals who have seen the need for change as they work in a practical fashion in nature. For instance, it has been realized that trees are dying in Europe not just because of air pollution but because forestry managements tidy up woodlands and take away the fallen branches, leaves, and dead trees that are needed to replenish the forest bed. It has been recognized that twenty percent of city waste is brush from urban forests that can be extracted, mulched, and reused. Steps are being taken to save wildlife of all types, to save so-called useless environments like wetlands, to discover why frogs are dying out, and so on. On every level, practical change is needed, and people are ready at the grass roots with the necessary ideas, energy, and enthusiasm.

We are in an interim period between casting off old values and finding new ones. One "new" value is the acknowledgment that everything, whether we call it living or dead, good or bad, has a part to play in the scheme of things, and should be accepted and loved for the life it is. Only when we, who have the most developed intelligence in physical form on Earth, become more balanced in our loving, can we be in a position to decide what is best for the whole. We are the decision makers on Earth, and there are no rigid rules for us to follow. Nature is constantly changing, as are we. When we begin to put our human interest alongside the interests of other life, we can properly fulfill our role as gifted humans. Instead of being destroyers, we can be redeemers, bringing joy to ourselves and to the planet.

Exercise:

Use memory and imagination to return to the highest state you have experienced. In the love of that state focus on the soul aspect of whatever part of nature you would like to contact, remembering that species have group souls. Harmonize with the qualities there. Listen. Ask questions if you wish. Do not expect to receive messages such as this book portrays, for each one of us is unique. Just listen within for your own resonant note, for however spirit connects with you. Accept what comes. Give thanks. Later on, after the meditation, act on any suggestions given.

CHAPTER FIVE

NATIONAL IDENTITY

At Findhorn I discovered that human groups that have developed a unique identity have life on the inner, or soul, level, the angelic level. There I became aware of a "Sleeping Beauty" pattern that seemed to be waiting to be awakened. From within I was told that the angel of our small group, which we called the Angel of Findhorn, was coming into being. When I asked what to do about it, I was told to recognize its possibility, to give it love and do our work with love, which would build its energies. Gradually it came to life and became incorporated into our world and work. This was the beginning of my exploration into the angels of human groupings. The following story of connecting with Canada unveiled to me that our relationship with angels affects countries and, ultimately, the planet. I also began to understand that our sense of national identity could have a negative or positive effect on us and others. It is important to integrate these matters individually, so the love of God can flow in us freely, unimpeded.

Personal Connection with a Country

In the fall of 1976, after an absence of thirty-five years and in the company of a young friend, Freya, I came back to live in my own natal area—Ontario, Canada. I felt myself to be very different from the girl who had left during World War II. For one thing, I felt I was a citizen of the world and had outgrown the limitations of being a citizen of just one country. In common with the cultural bias of the time, I felt that to have any nationalistic tendencies was definitely outmoded and even wrong. I had long ago thrown away the idea that nationality was important, in spite of having been educated in the Victorian idea of patriotism and having been required to memorize Sir Walter Scott's poem "The Lay of the Last Minstrel," which says, in part, "Breathes there the man, with soul so dead, / Who never to himself hath said, / This is my own, my native land!" Nationality had been used for divisive and destructive purposes in my opinion. We have been national robots, and I would have nothing to do with it. As if to prove my independence, I had obtained a passport issued by the Planetary Citizens' organization, though such planetary passports are not legally accepted.

In my homeland, it began to puzzle me that I was continually finding fresh joy in being in the area where I had grown up and where my family had lived for generations. I found I was loving the climatic extremes, which were so exhilarating after the continual rain of Britain and the continual sunshine of California. I had missed the wondrous little wildflowers that spring up in the Canadian woods before the leaves open; they seemed to have a radiance and purity greater than that in any garden or in transplanted flowers. For me there were no apples or peaches as tasty as those grown on the Niagara peninsula. The physical environment was familiar and brought up memories. The history and behavior of the people were familiar and comfortable, though I decided the provincial atmosphere had been improved by the immigration of Asians and Africans.

Even recent changes had meaning. For example, shortly after settling in Toronto I went to a concert in a hall named after Edward Johnson, who had been a friend of my father's. Near where I used to live in Toronto was a huge new library building called John Robarts Library, and I had been to university with John Robarts. I seemed to have links and memories wherever I went and whatever I did.

The Soul and Identity of a Country

I began to wonder why I kept recognizing my background connections. Was a national identity relevant in this day and age? If my assumption of a divine essence at the core of everything was valid with regard to a country, I could ask that question of the national angel. I attuned to the essence of Canada, the soul or angel of the country, and encountered an energy with enormous and vast purity, perhaps paralleling the broad, untouched lands of Canada. The angel conveyed to me that it could not properly perform its job of serving the country because the people had little sense of identity, and it had to work through people.

I knew from previous experience that the angelic world has not the sense of separateness that humans have and is a unified world always concerned with the good of the whole planet. Therefore I need not worry about the usual narrow self-promoting nationalism. I wondered if, after all, my background and my Canadianism was something deeper than I had wanted to recognize. Because I did not want to block the angel, I decided to explore the question of national identity with others. Freya and I coordinated two workshops that were attended by native-born and immigrant Canadians. We realized that the specifics of any identity are found through comparison. For that purpose we chose to compare ourselves with our big neighbor, the United States. Since I had been away from Canada for many years, I could see my native land with fresh eyes.

Our two workshops explored the concept of national identity by exchanging observations of the two countries and by attuning to the spiritual energies of our country. We concurred with the angel: the outstanding Canadian characteristic is that we don't know who we are. This has been true throughout our history. The only thing we agree on is that we are not Americans! In an attempt to be open-minded, I wondered if the answer was for Canada to join the United States. I asked the Angel of the United States if it considered this a good idea. "No," it intimated, "North America needs the balance that Canada gives." In my understanding, one example of this balance is in the use of freedom. America has been a wonderful bastion of freedom for the world. The Statue of Liberty is a great symbol of America welcoming and offering liberty to millions of people from many countries. But freedom, like anything, can be taken to an extreme. For the United States today, it has come to mean freedom without restrictions—freedom, for example, to buy as many guns as desired. Canada has offered a different way of dealing with freedom and with violence: by curtailing the sale of guns through laws.

We realized that Canadians have tended to settle their problems by means of law courts and government legislation. This spirit probably stems from the thousands of Loyalists, the Tories, who, more often than not, left the thirteen colonies because they simply disapproved of change by violence. They emigrated to British North America in order to live by their beliefs. Canadian history exhibits this peaceable and ordered approach. As an example, the Northwest Mounted Police was founded in 1873 to prevent in the developing Canadian West the violent lawlessness occurring in the American West. The Mounties controlled gun distribution and became a national symbol. For good or ill, government has played a major role in Canadian development and in supporting business. The United States expanded westward via railways built by private enterprise; the Canadian government sponsored its westward railways. Numerous white papers indicate that change continues to be initiated through government. Growth in the United States has unfolded very differently.

In spite of similar cultures, we began to find other differences. Instead of deliberately mixing populations into one homogeneous whole, like the people of the United States, Canada has had a policy of supporting differences. It has been described as a mosaic rather than a melting pot. Ignoring indigenous cultures, the backbone of modern Canada derives from French and British heritages, and Canada has come far, however it has bumbled, as a country of two cultures. Moreover, both cultures feel strongly Canadian. Canada is home. There is no feeling of France or Britain being the mother country, as there has been for, say, Algerian or New Zealand settlers. If this country had joined the American union, there is little doubt that the French culture would have virtually disappeared, as it has in Louisiana.

Another point of identity for Canadians is a great love of wilderness. Spacious, untouched wilderness areas have a powerful, pure energy that draws us and, if we let it, faces us with the basics of nature and ourselves. In most countries there is little virgin land. In the United States it is almost impossible to get away from the sight or sound of civilization, yet most Canadians can easily reach almost-untouched land and benefit from the peace found there.

Other qualities that make Canada unique emerged from our group interactions, qualities that seem unconnected with the land, yet consistent throughout Canadian history. Our very lack of identity makes us nonthreatening and therefore safe to confide in. When I left Canada during World War II to work in the United States for British employers, Americans would complain to me about the stuck-up Limeys, and the British would moan about brash Yanks. I automatically defended the attacked country. The same characteristic comes out when Canada plays the role of peacemaker.

As part of our comparison process in the workshops, we had an esoteric astrological chart done for both countries. The charts confirmed our own findings. According to the system used, there are energies—rays—that influence the soul and the personality aspects of every country. America is influenced from the personality level by what is termed the Sixth Ray, specifically the qualities of dedication and devotion, resulting in the big heart of American liberty and the fanaticism typified by McCarthyism. Canada's personality is said to be influenced by the Seventh Ray energies of administration, order, and ceremony, exemplified by its orderly cities and regimented attitudes.

People in many countries do not have to search for an identity. But Canada decided on a national flag, a national anthem, and a Charter of Rights only after World War II. Canadian schoolchildren are not trained to salute a flag or repeat a pledge. I have mentioned examples of Canadian lack of identity, because exploring a lack can lead to a change of values and interesting conclusions, as was the case in our workshops. However, in some countries, the search for recognition of an identity has shaken the world, causing numerous conflicts and wars, which have not yet been resolved.

⌘ INSIGHTS

1. Planetary Perspective

We realized in the workshops that none of us can have much idea of our national behavior until we leave our country either physically or psychically. Otherwise we continue to swim in a sea of patterned resonance, not realizing there might be other creatures who live in different waters and have different values. A planetary outlook is essential for accurate evaluation. This viewpoint was also expressed in the one significant book I found dealing with national identity: Rudolf Steiner's *Mission of the Folk Souls.* I like Steiner's approach, as he deals with the angelic hierarchy as forces, energies. Steiner wrote that people cannot possibly be of use to their own locale or country unless they are what he referred to as "homeless," which I might call a planetary citizen. Without a planetary perspective, one continues to make the same old mistakes, to fulfil the same old patterns that have always limited the country. We have reached a stage on the planet when we must communicate across cultural barriers. Understanding internationally does not imply that one must personally know different cultures. It means that we are no longer tied to acting according to our cultural norms, and we stop reacting to and judging other races. If we are so immersed in our race psyche that we cannot see beyond it, then we perpetuate the sort of behavior that has given nationalism its bad name. A universal citizen appreciates other cultures, delights in their ideas, and enhances the spiritual worth and value of all cultures. Yet we also need what we have acquired in our country, for we serve it poorly if we know nothing or little about it. To achieve some sort of balance, we need to honor our past; we are shallow and unintelligible without it. We need to perceive our role or the role of our own country from planetary viewpoints.

One could be a "national" of more than one country—a test of that might be if one feels a sense of belonging when a national anthem is sung. I myself felt aligned with three countries: with my native Canada, with Scotland (my main ethnic background, and where I felt comfortable from the moment of arriving), and with the United States. The sense of belonging to the United States arose in a strange way. In 1976 my American friends decided to do something to celebrate the American Bicentennial. They jokingly told me that I couldn't take part because I wasn't American, and in any case my ancestors had backed the wrong horse by deciding to migrate from there to Canada, becoming United Empire Loyalists. I took their joking seriously and was hurt; I didn't see why I couldn't participate in their celebrations. At that time I happened to contact a cousin who was living in California, and she, being a historian, talked about what strong ties the family had with the United States and how often members returned. I asked what the strong ties were, and she said "Washington." That didn't mean anything to me, until she explained that George Washington's mother, Mary Ball, was an ancestor. My grandmother was a Ball of the same family. In Revolutionary times the family had split, some remaining in America and some leaving. On hearing of this relationship, somehow all my hurt left me. I felt a new affiliation to the country and didn't care what anyone said. I did find, however, that when some American action grated on me, I returned to my Canadianness! Being nonjudgmental at all times is difficult!

Rudolf Steiner also said that in a past age the keynote, written on the temple at Delphi, was "Man, know thyself, and you will know the universe and the gods," and that the keynote now was to know ourselves as folk souls, national selves. This is, indeed, a far cry from the current assumption that nationality is a negative concept, but it makes sense as we expand into larger groupings. Having only a planetary awareness is like trying to function only from the soul level and omitting the personality. We have to balance all parts of ourselves, and it is no accident that our souls chose to be born in a certain geographical area or cultural context. Steiner also said that the Spirit of the Age gives guidance for the unfolding of the planet through the archangels (national angels), the angels being our intermediaries to the archangels. In other words, if we want to work for the planet, direction for that comes through national soul energies. Although the nation state is becoming outdated because of multinational business and concerns, at present the divine essence that represents one part of the whole is the angel of the country. And angels are very open to change. The planet is calling for humans to function in a new grouping, which is not loss of identity but rather greater identity.

2. Honoring Ethnic Origin

Before we began our workshops, we did not know that sociologists had discovered that:

> Ethnic differences, even in the second half of the twentieth century, proved far more important than the differences in philosophy or economic systems. Men who would not die for a premise or a dogma would more or less cheerfully die for a difference rooted in ethnic origins (Greeley, 1969). (p. 3)[1]

---

1. As quoted in McGoldrick, Monica, John K. Pearce and Joseph Giordano, *Ethnicity and Family Therapy*, New York: Guildford Press, 1982. From Greeley, A.M., *Why Can't They Be Like Us?* New York: Institute of Human Relations Press, 1969.

I hadn't thought much about ethnic origins, though it is clear that ethnic values and identification are retained for many generations, else I would not have made myself familiar with Maclean clan tartans and history. I had not realized that culture forms our meaning and also creates a certain order out of seemingly chaotic influences.

Steiner said that people are able to offer a free and positive contribution to evolution only if they understand their ethnic origin. This was the understanding that we in our workshop were coming to and that the angel indicated. Most of us hadn't bothered about our roots, and some of us didn't want to think about them; we wanted just to forget them. Their importance is emphasized in *Ethnicity and Family Therapy*:

> Ethnicity is a powerful influence in determining identity. A sense of belonging and of historical continuity is a basic psychological need. We may ignore it or cut it off by changing our names, rejecting our families and social backgrounds, but we do so to the detriment of our well being. (p. 5)

Only by accepting the whole of ourselves, which includes all facets of our makeup, do we feel complete and invulnerable, capable of not reacting to attack. Our ethnic origin is expressed in us unconsciously, and it is well to bring this to the surface. We can accept our roots, study them according to our interest, and see what that teaches us about ourselves. I think the concept of accepting our past is the basis for what we Westerners have called ancestor worship in other cultures. Ancestor worship seems a ridiculous practice to us, but if understood as acceptance and appreciation of our cultural and genetic heritage, it is a valid concept.

Recent studies have found, to quote from *Ethnicity and Family Therapy* again, that:

Ethnicity describes a sense of commonality transmitted over generations by the family and reinforced by the surrounding community. It is more than race, religion, or national and geographic origin.... It involves conscious and unconscious processes that fulfill a deep psychological need for identity and historical continuity (Giordano & Giordano, 1977). Ethnicity patterns our thinking, feeling, and behavior in both obvious and subtle ways. It plays a determining role in what we eat, how we work, how we relax, how we celebrate holidays and rituals, and how we feel about life, death and illness.

We see the world through our own "cultural filters"... (Watzlawick, 1976).

The subject of ethnicity evokes deep feelings, and discussion frequently becomes polarized or judgmental. According to Greeley, using presumed common origin to define "we" and "they" seems to touch on something basic and primordial in the human psyche. Similarly, Irving Levine has observed: "Ethnicity can be equated with sex and death as a subject that touches off deep unconscious feelings in most people."

Ethnicity is a powerful influence in determining identity. (pp. 4–5)

All of this is true on the personality level. As we become aware that we are prejudiced, the door opens to letting prejudice go. As we become loving, we see differently, for our personalities are freer. Put in another context, every individual, whether mineral, plant, animal, human, or beyond, has a background in which that individual is integrated structurally and functionally. For us all, these backgrounds, or patterns, stem from the qualities chosen by our soul for its expression and learning.

3. Becoming Aware of Our Behavior Patterns

For me a central core of the findings of our workshops was the realization of how little we are aware of acting within the boundaries of our national identity. Through the years I had perceived how nationals of other countries were easily recognizable owing to various mannerisms. While I was in England during World War II, I could spot an American from behind because of the walk, or Swedes from the way they would bow. Such things were obvious and funny, but unlike the rest of the world I, of course, didn't act in any but the normal way! Yet from childhood I remember that when my family would go for a drive and pull up at some garage for gas, the attendant would come forward and say to my father, "What would you like, Mac?" My father had never been to Scotland, but he obviously carried his genetic or cultural inheritance with him.

There is honor and necessity in being what one is, but when we are unaware of our behavior, when we don't know that our unique cultural background may appear peculiar, funny, or even barbaric to other eyes, then we unintentionally offend. This is true even in small matters. What is polite in one culture can be rude in another. In China a burp is a polite sign that the food is enjoyable. The smile of a Japanese may have a meaning different from a Western smile, a meaning of embarrassment instead of enjoyment. International understanding and agreement is un-likely if we all continue to remain stuck in our own cultures.

Personal mannerisms may offend others, and what likelihood is there of person-to-person understanding if many of our own characteristics are unknown to us and bubble up regardless? To me it is vital that I know what I am; otherwise I am swayed willy-nilly by my subconscious. Even if I don't like being proved wrong in any of my assumptions, I would rather face them than go around innocent of how I can grate on others. I don't want to be the robot of my behavior patterns. When I am aware of my behavior, I can deal with it and grow. To remain locked in a pattern is to be dead, crystallized, which can lead to devastating results. The war in Ireland is an example of old grievances passing from generation to generation without change. Besides being tragic, it can also be ridiculous, as in the case of an Irish Guardsman I knew in World War II. From neutral Ireland he had signed up to fight the war for England, yet he continually talked against the English as the enemy.

Becoming aware of these patterned behaviors is so important that I raised the subject in workshops I was leading. At first I was frustrated with the vacant stares I was given in response, but I realized that some things, like our noses, are so close we cannot see them. Recognition of the unconscious or suppressed areas of ourselves is now surfacing as personal stresses send us to psychological counselors. Perhaps as we travel more and as more non-Europeans settle in North America, we will see different ways of behaving and be given opportunities to change our own ways. But we do exhibit strong resistance to recognizing evidence or experience that challenges the adequacy of our hidden belief system. We all have blank spots in our perception of ourselves, and they are *danger spots*. I want to know mine; I want to choose how I live, to be as free and unlimited as possible so that love can flow out, and to fit into a changing world. Using our national uniqueness as a way to become aware of and serve both the planet and our nation seems a worthwhile aim and could obviate some needs to go to psychologists.

There are areas of our personality that we accept as so right that they, too, can become stumbling blocks. This was made clear to me by a story I heard about people's behavior on the island of Erraid. This island has been given over to the use of the Findhorn Foundation by its Dutch owners for eleven months of the year. The Foundation developers had to be very careful when relating to the nearby Mull islanders, on whom they depended for help in various areas. The islanders had their own background and life-style and were not very open to strange "New Age" folk. The British people from Findhorn were very careful when relating to the islanders and succeeded in establishing a fairly good relationship. Then a delightful California couple visited, and when meeting the islanders threw their arms about them and hugged them. Such demonstrative behavior was unpalatable to the islanders, who drew back in horror. In this situation, what was an attractive characteristic in America was considered repellent in another region. We have to be sensitive enough not to behave automatically according to our own backgrounds.

Gaining Wholeness

What was most important in our workshop groups was that we gained a sense of ourselves, and a happiness in being what we were. We realized that we did share unique characteristics and came to understand that these characteristics could be used positively or negatively. The very lack of identity in Canadians that makes us good confidants, peacemakers, and bridge builders also gives us a feeling of low self-worth. When recognized, any characteristic can be used appropriately in a situation; if it goes unrecognized, it uses *us* instead of our choosing its use.

The viewpoint that personal characteristics are in themselves neutral, neither good nor bad, had been brought home to me through the study of Personology, a system of thought that identifies the different inherent personal characteristics an individual is born with, mainly by measurements of facial distinctions. Personology helps individuals know and appreciate their own makeup, their "trait patterns." It also helps one see how any trait can be a help or a hindrance, depending on how one uses it. For instance, the trait of critical perception and an inclination to be exacting can be a wonderful advantage in a job requiring those qualities, such as accounting—but stay clear of a situation needing lots of tolerance, such as being a public relations officer! Or we can work on what we consider a weakness until it becomes a strength. Demosthenes corrected his stammer by practicing speech, eventually becoming Greece's leading orator. We always have choices as to how we use our dispositions, and it has been found that many physical characteristics change with a change in behavior.

Most of the people who attended these workshops went through a liberating process. Besides bringing to light our commonalities—I discovered what a typical Canadian I am—we found uniting and uplifting factors previously unrecognized. For instance, one immigrant Canadian had been in the country for twelve years, but because she still felt part of and proud of the land of her birth, she felt guilty about her acceptance of Canadian amenities. When she realized that adding her culture was natural in a multicultural country and enhanced its richness, she felt free for the first time to honor both cultures. Another member of our group had been on the battleground of the two basic Canadian cultures all her early life, being a child of the only English-speaking family in a Quebec village. She saw no answer to these cultural difficulties—"the two solitudes" as they have been called—until it came as a revelation to her that a country had a unifying factor, a soul, through which could be resolved the long enmities that had shaped her life and limited her outlook.

Later on I gave a workshop in Quebec at the height of a period of separatist fervor. Most participants were separatists—teachers, artists, professionals. The group were united in their interest and desire to put love first in their lives. Somehow the subject of politics arose, and the fur began to fly. Then the group realized, almost as a revelation, that they were approaching the situation with rampant emotionalism, and they paused. When one of the group eventually suggested that perhaps what we should do was lend our energies to the whole, asking that God's will be done in the situation, we had the most powerful group meditation I had ever experienced. We did not denigrate the French-Canadian identity; on the contrary, we realized that French Canada was leading the rest of the country in becoming aware and strong in its identity, after more than two centuries of being the butt of prejudice. Also, French Canada had a leading creative role to play in the country. As a group, too, we found that our solutions were individual. As we individually attuned to our own wholeness, our strength, we no longer needed to be defensive. Then, secure in ourselves, we could look out in an objective fashion and be capable of dealing with problems on broader issues.

Of course, linguistic differences are not the only divisive factors. I held a workshop in Alberta at a time of strong separatist feeling based on economic, political, and regional differences with the federal government. As a group, we came to the realization that the powerful sense of needing to separate was based on our emotional reactions and that we were not putting into practice our expressed personal beliefs in loving behavior.

Again, the grievances were not artificial, but we were not deal-ing with them in a holistic way. By attuning to the angel of the area, we received unemotional and global perspectives. It was a case of thinking globally and acting locally.

Background Influences

We often use our backgrounds negatively. When I was in Germany some years ago, I found a whole generation of youths wanting to repudiate the Nazi past, which is an understandable attitude but unrealistically ostrich-like. It is important that we recognize the shadow side of national characteristics as well as individual qualities, a point Carl Jung made. Since that time, there has been a resurgence of Nazism, a glorification of the shadow side. As always, we need to find a balance. There has been a wave of denigration of the past in many countries, which is rather like throwing the baby out with the bath water. In America, in reaction to the belief that the American way of life is the best in the world, the feeling arose after the Vietnam War that America is a selfish, consuming monster that has ruined peoples, the environment, and the resources of the world. This view departed sharply from recognition of the sterling qualities of the Founding Fathers. In Canada I came across a repudiation of the Victorian past without an acknowledgment of the many positive aspects of that era—which, in any case, was how the world was then, and fortunately is not now. We cannot expect the past to have the values that have since evolved, but it is ben-eficial to recognize and appreciate the relevant values and keep those of our choice. Unless we accept and embrace all aspects of ourselves and of our countries, there are vulnerable gaps leading to explosive consequences, and we will not be whole.

I came across one interesting example of the influence of racial background. Deepak Chopra writes that in California

Japanese-Americans continued to have low rates of heart disease, regardless of the cholesterol levels of their blood, when they retained strong ties to Japanese culture. What kept these men healthy was a social bond, a programmed awareness. Social bonding takes place at the level of mind, where you share a larger self, an interconnected psyche that is as sensitive and intricate as an individual psyche.[2] Chopra seemed to me to be relating how the physical body continues to be influenced by our heritage.

Purpose in Contacting National Souls

The idea of responding to the angel of a country is not prevalent. Recently there has been a revival of interest in angels helping in individual human affairs, but I have not come across interaction with the biblical "principalities" or angels of large groupings. In the next chapter I mention some occasions in which contacting such an angel was helpful to me.

It was useful to find clarity about my own country. When I first contacted the soul of Canada to question if there was a need for Canadian unity, I perceived that the distinctness that is Canada, with its particular experiment in group entities, had a role to play in world service. Later I was asked not to be defeatist about its situation. The angel explained that the country needed heart power, needed its people to enjoy it. More recently, the soul of Canada told me that it would be better for Canada to remain united and cease diverting its energies into federal versus provincial affairs, yet what was most important was that individuals find their own divine cores. If the bonds of understanding and sympathy are not extended from one person

---

2. Chopra, Deepak. *Ageless Body, Timeless Mind.* New York: Bantam New Age Book, 1989.

to another, but instead decrease, which is a human choice, then political or geographical division may be the way to learn. But at this time, when people are becoming more global, harmony and charity still begin best at home.

Here I want to say that in my experience, the angelic realm is entirely nonpolitical and nonjudgmental. The angels see that we live in a bewildering world of doubt and convoluted thinking, but such is not their world. The energies they use are not limited to the dimensions of human intellectual preoccupations and emotional experiences. They are very aware of the qualities that we possess and express, and they see how vitally important it is that each of us align our personalities with our souls in order to have a greater perspective. Attuning to the angels also always helps us in that it takes us to a more joyful and peaceful realm.

I was concerned about mentioning angels publicly, thinking that it might do more harm than good, but the Angel of Canada repeated that the angelic realm should not be glossed over, that recognition by many was around the corner and was necessary. It told me not to worry in that respect, that worrywarts are not effective! It asked me to emphasize love of the land, something we all had in common. Because this is often not appreciated, it needs to be brought to the forefront. The angel expressed its need of our love and optimism.

Other Angelic Aspects

The qualities of national angels, like those of humans, differ according to surrounding situations. It was a joy to go to the Canadian West and find qualities of the angel other than ones I had previously known: a greater openness, for instance. I realized what a great variety of energies national angels mold and that certain energies are uppermost in different geographical area. Through the years various questions arose that caused me to link with other aspects of the angelic realm. In 1982 I was concerned with the plight of North American Indians and attuned to their angel. It said that just as the Canadian oversoul had difficulty in functioning through Canadians who had no identity, so it had difficulty in functioning through Indians who were bitter. Native peoples have every reason to be bitter after the treatment they have received for centuries, but holding on to resentment nevertheless is a block to their linking with the soul level. Their angel conveyed that it was a difficult period for them, but that difficulty is diminishing—no doubt as both we and they see, accept, and honor their contribution to the whole.

There are also unique large and small geographical areas that have their own angels. I have always found angels of islands to have very distinctive identities; they are as self-contained as possible in the unity of the angelic realm. One such was the Angel of Manitoulin, a large island in Lake Huron. It had a strong, eager, Native Canadian presence. It told me that the island was a sacred place that acted as a reminder to humans to achieve, innovate, and experiment both in ideas and in the concrete realm.

At the Kingston Peninsula in the Maritimes, the angel seemed to be linked to and identified with the land in a new way; it explained that it was experimenting with a close association there, something that rarely happened in the Americas, a different sort of blending. Perhaps that new blending was what I later came across in the plains of China, where the human and the angelic presence was as one, a unity I believed came from thousands of years of recognizing each other and working together.

Need for Planetary Awareness and Change

We know that our culture inevitably shapes each of us. Without it we would be nonentities with no base for behavior. The conscious and unconscious beliefs and assumptions that shape our conduct and mold us early in life can be changed. We need no longer be brainwashed to perceive the world the way people in our culture perceive it. Our biased reality, the limitations of our cultural tendencies, our rigidity, our unconscious beliefs that are a fundamental cause of many of the world's problems probably influence us more than our conscious beliefs. The assumption of our societies that their way of life is the best and that others should be made to conform, by force if necessary, no longer fits in with planetary development.

If we wish to change our collective unconscious beliefs, our cultural DNA, we encounter strong resistances. We have all developed certain habits, ways of thinking and acting, that have become automatic. We do not easily alter our grooves. We don't like change. I well remember a friend whose job it was to initiate new office systems. Invariably he was hated and resisted by the office staff. But if our beliefs are unconscious, then how can we possibly change them? One approach, taken by psychologists and other counselors, is to help us become more aware by recognizing our repressed emotions and thoughts. And life itself always gives us specific opportunities, as it did for me when returning to Canada.

Experiences with the essence of larger groupings continue to be relevant. All nations are part of the planet, and national borders do not stop environmental pollution. In any case, nationalism is a modern development, arising in Europe with the Age of Reason. Some say the nation-state is not in decline; it remains rooted in the soil and hearts of its people. Present national policies are being affected by the needs of multinational corporations. Because of this global reach on the part of business, the need for a planetary awareness is increasing.

We aso need to realize that we cannot understand other nations unless we understand our own. When we have accepted ourselves and our own race, we are at peace with ourselves and no longer on the defensive. Then we are not threatened by others and can open up to them. As the German philosopher Count Hermann Keyserling suggested, we can perhaps see other nations as functions and expressions of one great, indivisible man. Heightened awareness of other cultures leads to the conclusion that there is beauty, significance, richness, and expansion of the human spirit in the diversity of the world's cultures. Cultures emerge as a blossoming of genius and have local habitations. Distinctive national characteristics may be regenerated by contact with other traditions or may blend with different energies to produce new flowerings.

There is a constant ferment of ethnic groupings wishing to become nations, in the old Soviet Union, in Yugoslavia, in Africa, and elsewhere. Canada continually seems on the point of splitting. Such events may appear to be a step backward into old patterns. However, as individuals claim their whole selves on all levels, we prepare for a greater unity. The positive aspect of this outbreak of identity-claiming is that it is part of a necessary knowing of ourselves and of experiencing democracy. In this rash of nationalism it is more important than ever that our great inner identity be claimed, that we know God within. Only when we are at peace with it can we step beyond ethnicity—we can always find that greater identity from wherever we are, thanks to God's grace. I see the current crises as understandable searches for individuality; the surfacing of repressions, old hates, and problems are necessary steps toward equilibrium. One cannot create unless simultaneously one destroys former creations; the power of balance then emerges. It is interesting that in Europe, where nationhood has been in existence for the longest time, the trend is to greater unity, that those with experience as democratic nations are choosing federation. It is a slow process, but the speed of change has increased immensely and will continue to do so. It is almost as if there is a breakdown in our immune system, which we have needed to develop variety, and now we are becoming more open to one another, gaining access to new states of consciousness.

There is no one way to learn of another culture. Travel, reading, ingenuity, intelligence, loving openness, all help. Necessity is another incentive. Up to now humanity has been acquisitive and exploitive rather than cooperative, but now the world is calling for a planetary society and seems almost hell-bent that we get the message. Love is inexorable. We change the world as we change our assumptions. All countries have the polluted planet as a universal symbol of the need to change. To achieve global harmony and a sustainable planetary society, we don't have to alter human nature, only our unconscious programming. We must consciously identify with our true nature, with the love that we are. We need the meaning that traditional cultures offer. Culture is a practical necessity, a body whose disciplines are everyone's business. Distinctive national characteristics need not be erased and, in fact, may be regenerated by contact with other traditions. The balancing principle will in due time bring the world to greater cooperation and greater individual liberty.

Buried at the heart of every great civilization is love, and each culture has a universal mission, a different set of qualities to offer to the whole. Our individual, national, and global tensions are pressuring us to move to peace and harmony within and without, and to play our part in this decisive time in our world's evolution.

Exercise:

Again, attune within to the highest state that you know, and in the love and joy of that state focus on the love and joy of the angel of your country. Stay in touch with the vibrations of your country as you are aware of them at that moment. Be sensitive to its qualities. Be open to its intelligence. If you wish, ask how you can best serve your country.

Each of us tunes into a different quality of the country because each of us has a unique viewpoint. And all countries encompass many qualities. I find different aspects coming to mind at different times and in different places in a country. It is therefore helpful to compare your experience with that of a friend, if possible. We can always help our country by lending our energy to whatever comes to us at a given time, and we can add our country to the list of those we pray for in our regular meditations.

⌘ CHAPTER SIX

SOULS OF COUNTRIES

In the last chapter I told of my first exploration of and connection with the soul of a country. This chapter is about other countries and more general facets of national characteristics. I find the perspectives of the angels of countries not only interesting and helpful but also indicative of present planetary changes. Though I learned much about myself and cultural values in my explorations into the soul of my native land, attuning to the soul of other countries was a further learning process. It is difficult, if not impossible, to fully understand a foreign country, another race psyche or collective attitude, for years of living in our own country have bred in us certain assumptions and perspectives that we take for granted as correct. Another country's assumptions are just different. However, attunement to the essence level is possible and is always a tremendous help, for the spirit of God is there and the inner core of everything is based on love.

National characteristics are developed through many factors: history, education, culture, geography, climate. Any section of land has an identity, and national characteristics are seen in many places. For example, architecture shows national characteristics—Greek, Italian, Spanish, German—and, in turn, emphasizes national dispositions. Churchill urged that the chambers of the House of Commons bombed during World War II be rebuilt as before, saying that our buildings shape us. I believe that a student entering the college grounds of Oxford or Cambridge is influenced by the structures.

The French-American bacteriologist René Dubos wrote that just as biological diversity facilitates Darwinian evolution, so cultural diversity is essential for social progress. He thought it fortunate that all over the world ethnic and regional groups were asserting their identity and beginning to recapture a measure of autonomy. He thought it might help increase cultural diversity and thereby the rate of creative social change. In *So Human an Animal* he also wrote: "Precisely because antecedent social forms still condition the development of all aspects of civilization, each part of the world tends to retain its cultural identity, despite the fact that raw material, technological practice and power equipment exhibit such uniformity all over the world." Dubos contrasted the traditions of urban development symbolized by the French (Swiss-born) architect Le Corbusier, who was influenced by classical European traditions of apartment dwellings in compact cities, with the American architect Frank Lloyd Wright, who expressed the pastoral tradition of America in single-family houses.

In one way or another, all of us can be affected by the spirit of a foreign country on various levels. Although at first I had received inner inspiration on many subjects, which I put into words, as time went by my attunements went deeper and became quality experiences more difficult to verbalize, or else words felt unnecessary. Inner revelations bolstered my confidence and trust in spiritual realms, but I was always seeking their relevance to everyday living. I needed to accept the idea that attuning to the soul of a country made sense. An open mind is a step in the process of growth, evoking and bringing to consciousness a greater wholeness. As I became more centered, I began to graduate from being just a learner to being a helper, to being creative. I began to attune to a country and direct love to it, or to some aspect of it.

I remember that when I was in Ottawa, Canada's capital, I attuned to the angel there and found it was in a cage that prevented it from working freely. This cage had been built by all the negative thoughts of Canadians toward politics. I myself had considered politics an unscrupulous business and thoroughly disliked it. Now I realized that I had helped build that cage. This was my opportunity to change and to choose to send love to the political situation, the governing of the country—not necessarily to the politicians. All countries need such strengthening. Angels of countries seek to influence and aid through humans and certainly can use any helpful energies we provide them.

I had another example on my first visit to Hawaii in 1976. The Angel of Hawaii told me that it sought to temper American materialism and was spinning a new dream for visionary hearts. It felt that it had made a start with this vision, for visitors often returned to their own countries with a new tolerance toward other peoples. In a subsequent inner contact, the angel was spiraling energies in and out, and my love seemed to help smooth the movement.

On a trip I took around the world in 1983 to give talks and workshops, one of my aims was to attune to the soul or angel of different countries to see if any significant patterns would emerge. I received support for this endeavor from the Soul of Holland, which conveyed to me that to expand knowledge of the souls of countries is a worthwhile endeavor. According to it, national energies have had to work with humans who are unconscious of them, and it makes a tremendous difference to them if we recognize and willingly blend with the harmonies they are trying to bring about on our levels. Conscious human cooperation with planetary plans makes a wonderful dance of what might seem to be only pressures, and those who can keep in step are at the beginning of a new movement of growth in human awareness.

The Angel of Scotland mentioned that established networks, like that of the old British Commonwealth and of the Scottish clan system, still play a part by helping people keep ties with their roots even when moving to new lands. They have been useful models for building on the past. New networking forms will not be so established and rigid; Findhorn is a prototype of this. The angel said that my attempt in this book to describe a culture with its changing energy is a delicate task. Generalizations are too simple, yet the feel of a culture and its energy are simple. The angel indicated that emphasis on the positive is still important, because we cannot build from negative forces.

The Soul of India I could contact easily, no doubt because of the customary openness of its people to spiritual ideals. In this period, with India seeking to find a new balance in the modern world, there are many new energies at play and bringing about changes, which is confusing because of the similarity between old and new teachings. A great new factor for world unity and continuity could emerge in India; confirmation of individual power and wholeness is a key. The angel seemed to be lifting people up and shaking them, as if to startle them out of ruts, but with tremendous love and dedication.

In New Zealand I noticed that most of the original tree growth had been felled for sheep runs and that most replanting had been of foreign tree species. The tree energies told me that it is important for each area to have the strong energy of its own natural growth in order to embody its own uniqueness. Although exotic species could have value and the mingling of many varieties helps in the realization of oneness, the country could contribute best from a strong background of its own special plant growth.

The Angel of Australia was trying to lift the energies slowly, as if peace were needed. Its exuberant spirit would like to promote a greater sense of subtlety in the people. It seemed youthful, growing, moving, becoming more powerful. There was a sort of dark earthiness that had something to do with the aborigines and was holding back current Australian destiny. It seemed to me that the aboriginal people were not receiving the help necessary for them to live. Years ago, when I was telepathically linking with a network of people who were working for the "light," as we put it at the time, a group of aborigines was the easiest for me to contact. They were immediately present when I thought of them. Perhaps they function in subtle dimensions all the time. Later, to my delight, I accompanied an Australian aborigine on a tour for some days and took the opportunity to question him about his culture. We had a good rapport but, to my dismay, no intellectual exchange, for he did not respond or function on that level. When, more recently, I read that a group of aborigines had decided to stop incarnating on the planet, I could partly understand their choice.

A quartz-crystal deva in Australia suggested that it is important for us to get in touch with the intelligence of this land, which is linked with its ancientness. We can help raise its consciousness to a brighter and less heavy level. One difficulty is that its people feel the vigor to rush ahead regardless of obstacles, a sort of puppy force. I felt that the delicate energy of opal essence was working to refine sensibilities, to bring a softer influence and a more balanced perspective. I noted that the vast angelic opal energy is closely connected with the soul of the country in this particular work.

On returning to Canada after this world trip, I felt a sense of enthusiasm in its angel, an eagerness for Canadians to seek their destiny optimistically. At the same time I found the Angel of the United States had much creativity that was seeking an outlet; its people needed to be aroused. There seemed to be much for the United States to do in the world and a sense of frustration with which the angel was trying to cope.

Continuous Change

Because nations grow and change like all other life, I do sometimes wonder about the value of sharing perhaps outdated messages like these from 1983. And I, like all people, focus on what interests me. For example, I happen to like opals and often attuned to their soul level when I was in Australia, where they are mined. Attunements ten or twenty years later would find that both the country and we ourselves had changed and had different interests. I am simply sharing the process as it took place.

My relationship with the angelic energies has also changed, and I seem to be more at one with them, sometimes aware of them as different patterns of light and no longer receiving or needing specific information. For example, during my first contact with the Soul of South Africa in 1985, I "saw" strands of light extending from where I was to every corner of the country—separate strands like thread, not a diffuse light. Each one was glowing, radiating, shining, and they made a wonderful pattern where they all met. There was one large strand pulsating with energy from the vortex to me. I sent love back, and sparkler-like flashes of light were emitted, flashing out and landing everywhere in the country. Gradually that one strand grew and included many others, until all were linked in love in an umbrella pattern whose vortex shone more and more brightly until it was a great world light. Such light patterns continued in my inner soul contact with countries, though they were usually simpler than this one.

Besides these patterns, I experienced a great heart contact in South Africa. There I felt the soul energies as extraordinarily loving. From my initial contact with angels in Scotland, I had felt their love to be remote because, as I realized later, I had expected it to be focused on me, as human love is, whereas the focus was on the whole. As I came to realize that it was my limited expectations that had made it seem unloving, I learned to appreciate its vast outreach. In South Africa it seemed that the angel had learned more about love and compassion than is usual, perhaps because of the very difficulties in that country. It was embracing all of its peoples and soothing them. I realized that any of us can help that vast love by our individual love and trust in the present and future. Never before had I felt that the element of trust was so greatly needed. In a sense the angel was asking us to be co-creators with it, and to be all-embracing, as it was. In its understanding and compassion, it was the nearest to a personal human love that I had so far encountered. I gathered from it that we need not know the future or experience results, as we humanly hope to know and experience. We can just join in the loving, and speculation doesn't help.

It seemed to me then that South Africa could play an important planetary role. The country certainly had extreme problems, but finding a way to solve them would assist other countries. Everyone I met, admittedly mostly whites, was deeply concerned and dedicated to finding solutions. They reminded me of the people in Britain during World War II, when everyone was involved in the war effort and personal agendas didn't enter in. But in South Africa it was more like civil war, with other nations taking sides without knowledge of the situation. Of course, apartheid had to be abolished, but many complexities had to be considered. The poignant beauty of the land, of the young tribal children—who seemed to shine with a special radiance, perhaps because in tribal life all adults act as their parents—and of the animals affected me deeply. The angel was asking us to extend our boundaries and encompass much more in our love. Certainly it is love and not confrontation that is needed in that area. Since then, free elections have taken place without the feared bloodbath, and I believe the love of the humans and the angel greatly influenced this result.

Without Judgment

The heart connection with the soul of a country was also paramount when I first visited China in 1988 to 1989. We landed at Guilin at night, and my sight of Chinese soil somehow put me in touch with the angel. I picked up a feeling of deep, deep compassion, which stayed with me for several hours while I collected baggage, went through customs, drove to our destination, and ate a meal. Usually, when I have a feeling of compassion, it is momentary, and in a flash I return to normal. Here I experienced a new depth and persistence of love. This profound compassion arose because the angel knew of the difficulties that China had to undergo in order to change, of the almost insolvable tasks so many people would face to undergo in a short time a fundamental transformation from a very ancient civilization to a modern one. When I asked how I could best help with regard to all the difficulties we see in other nations, I was told to admit and accept them *without judgment*. Many mistakes would be made by the people as they reacted to the new energies. This perspective should have prepared me for the Tiananmen Square massacre several months later. Certainly, my awakened compassion and lack of prejudgment colored my approach to everything and everyone I met in China, giving me an openness and tolerance that nothing else could have achieved.

Local areas of course have their own uniqueness. The Angel of Guilin, an area that has traditionally been a creative refuge for artists, said that artists could still link with the incredible landscape in a holistic, subtle, artistic form of thought that stretches the mind—still poetic, but using metaphors that move and change and keep the mind alert without the need for intellectual knowledge of the past.

After my visit to China I remember reading an article about the need for individual freedom there, which the country, like much of Asia, is tasting through the adoption of capitalism, and also the need for authoritarian control to prevent waste, such control being part of the Chinese heritage that has derived from Confucianism. The reasoning was that capitalism is very much based on greed. Make what money you can, and sooner or later everyone will benefit. A gas station on every corner, so to speak, is all right if you can make money from it. China, with its vast population, cannot afford such an attitude; if most of the billion people in China owned cars, it would bring about utter disaster. What is needed is an awakening of a certain doggedness in the Chinese, which they can apply if they believe in the need for it. This calls for a leader who can awaken and feed the aspiration and pride of the people. The article made sense to me, and I was glad to read something that took the basic soul of a people into consideration. But what it mainly evoked was a desire to help. We can all help by sending out love to a situation, without envisioning any particular form.

Embrace Change

In 1989 to 1990, I visited Southeast Asia with a friend who had lived in various countries of that part of the world and led tours to introduce people to the arts, crafts, and religions of the area. En route I found the Japanese Angel in an intricate dance, dealing with the factors arising in a country where power comes and tests individuals. The angel was trying to rectify an insufficient awareness on the part of the Japanese of the needs of the rest of the planet. In Thailand, the angel said that things were changing very quickly in the world at that time and that the national angels were dealing with energies in a new way, releasing finer qualities in the knowledge that the effect on the material world would be vast. Old patterns had to change, and the angels were trying to minimize the fear and resistance that relinquishing the old brings, in order to cushion us humans and to proceed with their work. How we adjust to the new energies, which are shaped by the natural patterns of the country, is our choice. During another contact with the Thai Angel, I sensed a very lovely widespread energy, stretching out all around and, in particular, helping Cambodia. I felt that the Southeast Asian angels were more linked to one another than any I had experienced in the West.

Bali is an Indonesian island that I, like so many people, fell in love with. Its green terraced fields and tropical trees were a beautiful setting for a people to whom religion appeared to be as natural as breathing. Every home has its own temple, a separate place dedicated to worship, and every village has several temples that are in use and alive. All the Balinese seemed to be artistic, whether in what we call the arts and crafts or in how they live. I have always disliked ritual, for in our Western churches it seems to me meaningless repetition. In Bali I found a respect and love for ritual because of how it is lived there.

Their religion is deeply integrated into their culture. I found also a profound understanding of things spiritual.

The Angel of Bali I found to be more connected with its culture than any other I had known, and it seemed to understand other cultures. When I asked if it was concerned with modern commercialism, it answered that it did not particularly see a problem, that the best way to meet detrimental trends was to be its own whole self and let the trends work out according to the people's choice. The Balinese were still creative, it said, in what is their field. After meeting and listening to a wonderful traditional *ikat* (a type of weaving in which the threads are pre-dyed in order to create a pattern) weaver, who spent months or years creating a textile imbued with power for religious purposes, I asked the angelic world whether such selfless dedication would change. I was told that all share in the universal energies of the planet, and though dedication to their art may lessen in intensity, inspiration can broaden. The art may change but be no less rich—perhaps less precise, perhaps more uplifting. Modern methods can be used and the work charged with mighty blessing in a different way. Blessings need not die with change, as love grows. Some days later the Angel of Bali, which seemed especially warm and happy, having previously welcomed me through its people and their art, now welcomed me on the soul level. It said it tried to encircle all who came to the island with its love, in order to help us pick up its message of loving balance to distribute elsewhere and to celebrate life.

The angelic force of Indonesia, which had a turbulent and richly dressed feeling, as of old cultures (this, of course, from the personality aspect of the angel), was not responsive to me. It seemed to be too busy melding the various islands together. It was as if the entry of Western culture to the islands was its concern and it was experimenting to find an appropriate blend.

It was a time of inward turning for Indonesia, a time to be left alone to find that blend.

Staying Flexible

After Indonesia I visited for several weeks in Nepal with its fascinating mix of civilizations. First open to foreigners in 1951, by our Western standards it was at that time the fifth poorest country in the world and had practically no roads. People casually talked of walking for four or five days to get to the nearest village. And walking in Nepal is up and down, with no flat areas for catching one's breath! The first motor vehicle in Pokhara, the second-largest town, was taken there by plane in 1957. But culturally and in other ways it is exceedingly rich, with settings that look medieval to us, intricate architecture and images influenced by Buddhism and Hinduism. The many temples, pagodas, and stupas painted with great eyes, the divers statues and gods, the numerous little towns that had been kingdoms, the myriad traditions, were almost bewildering combinations to me.

The Angel of Nepal had a very happy energy, which was a joy to contact. There was a sense of archaic crowns and of rough edges. Again, in this time of change it was carefully feeling its way into the future. I asked if it would like its people to remain as they are—comparatively happy, isolated, and primitive—or to become modernized. I was told desire is not what matters, and Nepal is part of the changing world. So I asked what the angel considered the best way for change to come about. It said that there was no best way, no master plan, and that each situation had to be met as it arose. Unless people meet life with flexibility, we experience resistance and pain, through which we learn. In the angelic world there is no suffering; angels attempt to express purely whatever is theirs to do, and expressing purity requires extreme sensitivity. The strong winds of change on the planet, regardless of appearances, are changes bringing greater awareness. When I asked if it is important for us to realize that there are angels of countries, they answered affirmatively. Until all life harmonizes, there will be parts set against other parts, which in a body or a planet is disease.

The Himalayan mountains were conducive to inward turning, as the traditions of holy men living there have shown. It may be that there the grandeur of nature dwarfs the ego and looses the soul. I had planned to go trekking for a week, but a malfunctioning knee finally forced me to realize that trekking on the hilly terrain was not possible. So a week on my own at Pokhara, fairly immobile, was a wonderful opportunity for meditation. I took full advantage and reveled in attunements— to the mountains, clouds, hills, rivers, buffalo, butterflies, trucks, trekking, birds, lake, planet, my own questions. The awesome mountains seemed to hold planetary secrets, to be transforming powers, and I gained much clarity.

Before proceeding to Kashmir, I had the great joy of seeing the Taj Mahal, which more than met expectations. It is, indeed, a sublime expression of human love for a human being, and architects and craftsmen must have also attuned to the love and beauty. It has a tremendously uplifting effect and is considered such a monument to love that, though it is a mausoleum, it draws honeymooners. Since 85 percent of tourists to India visit there, it certainly seems to be doing a job for humanity.

Link Between People and Nature

In Kashmir we found long-standing political unrest and a curfew that limited movement to a couple of hours a day. We were staying on a stationery house boat, and were allowed only to be rowed around the lake in small boats, though floating vendors promptly found us in this tourist-starved area. I found the Angel of Lake Dal to be a very gracious, moving presence that, like so many in Asia, is more closely linked with humanity than its equivalent in North America, where lake devas or other nature beings are separate from and sometimes not even aware of people. Even the great mountains in these areas are linked with humans. Or maybe it is the other way around, that the people are linked with the environment. In much of Asia the natives, unlike the North American natives, have definitely changed the environment through the ages, especially in settled regions. The Angel of Kashmir indicated that the long lineage of gracious living in Kashmir would continue, as it had through past conquests, that the joint influence of the people, the land, the lakes, and the mountains had to be expressed in each individual and group. What I might see as negative from a short range is part of the process of change and learning. When I again asked how to help the situation, I was told to weave peace and love into it, and, though that might seem a trite and sugary method, it could be potent. As the American spiritual teacher Ram Dass has put it: totally involved, totally unattached.

Finding Balance Continuously

The next countries I visited in 1990 were Brazil and Argentina. Almost fifty years ago, during World War II, I had worked in South America and had encountered the Sufi approach to the spiritual world. I had not returned since. The contrasts between the two times were fascinating. I was continuing to learn to respond, to not react, and to send love at the same time. Therefore my attunements to the angelic world were not very informational, even if they were deeper. What I shared about my awareness of national identity and its connection to planetary change aroused great interest in both countries. I realized anew that it is not my job to talk about the special purpose or characteristics of a country, even if I know them. It is for the people to view their country or district from a holistic viewpoint, to discover the great loving energy of which they are a part, and to feel that they can use the energy constructively. Discovering our identity, accepting our mistakes, honoring our background, and aligning to our inner essence are how we discover our individual, national, or planetary way of life. Allowing ourselves to accept our past without judgment or regret removes stress. Always remember that life forever changes, and cultural change comes as individuals change. We must find balance in all things.

Brazil had a very present, forceful energy. I loved the lack of prejudice, which I remembered from my previous visit. I also realized more clearly that national characteristics are personality aspects of the oversoul or angel, resulting from qualities of the soul level. It is alignment to the soul level that connects us with a nation's true identity and keeps our perspective from becoming too narrow. Since my training and experience had been to align to spirit, I was inclined to be intolerant of the traits in the emotional and psychic domains. Here again I was learning their part in the whole.

Argentina's soul energy I first experienced as a beautiful, quiet sweetness, a great contrast to my personal reaction to the city of Buenos Aires, which looked as if it had gone backward in fifty years. The French-style architecture and broad avenues were shabby and crumbling, and the city did not have the bustling modernity of Brazilian cities. I was reminded by the angel that it is our creative awareness, not my personal views, that helps in any situation!

On a later visit to Argentina and Brazil, in 1995, I found that my connection with the angels varied in different places and times, or perhaps it was that I had changed. For example, while I was with a loving and united group in Argentina, the angel was very loving and emphasized the need for love to bridge differences. Later, in the big city of Buenos Aires, there seemed to be a block between me and the angel, which eventually broke open and let love come through very strongly. Such changing experiences seemed to be telling me to keep realigning and not come to conclusions.

When attuning to the Angel of Spain in 1995, I was aware that it was surrounded by a darkness that was trying to smother it. I felt that the darkness was ancient—the Inquisition came to mind. The angel struggled and struggled until it was finally free, at which point the darkness came together in human form, submitted, and bowed to the angel. There was a great sense of liberation.

While in four Andean countries in 1997, I was particularly interested in contacting the early cultures of the areas. The civilizations there seemed very colorful and ceremonial, evoking and working with the nature forces in a much more conscious way than we do in the West nowadays. At the pre-Incan complex at Tiahuanaco, Bolivia, there is evidence of equal value being accorded to both male and female deities, a unique attitude. The ancient people there seemed philosophical about their disappearance, saying that each civilization has its timing. But on the Island of the Sun in Lake Titicaca, Peru, I had the impression of sadness at the demise of the Incas. I also felt that the ancient people had a sense of the great privilege of living on this holy island of the Incas, and a feeling that the island still holds energies of value for a greater whole. At Sacsahuaman, the huge walled fortress of Incan Cusco, I also found sadness at the demise of the Incas, who were defeated there. Again, a feeling of closeness to nature and an appreciation that now people can take nature into account in their living and come to a new creation. At Machu Picchu, it seemed that the rugged, steep mountains and gorges in the floating mist provided channels for powerful nature influences, which can be tapped by humans and might be a reason for building a city in such an unlikely high place.

The angels of the four countries conveyed in general that they would be glad of human help but asked that we also help joyfully, because there are heavy energies in the lands. They requested that we focus not on the differences in each country, but seek unity in each and find people and situations to love in each. The angels would like to reach their people and have them realize the importance of contributing to their country, a request made by angels all over the world. My attention was arrested by the fact that in Colombia, which has a dark reputation, I met an unusually high number of people working from a spiritual point of view. A balancing act?

To Flow with Change

It seems that there is a ferment of change touching every country on our planet. On my return from my trip in 1990, I found even my stolid Canada again in the throes of an identity crisis, and the crisis continues. But global changes are not merely identity crises; they indicate fundamental changes in the human mindset. For example, in the economics of global corporations, national boundaries no longer play a critical role in defending economic horizons. I remember that George W. Ball, former U.S. Undersecretary of State, said that conflict will increase between the world corporation, which is a modern concept evolved to meet the requirements of the modern age, and the nation state, which is still rooted in an archaic concept unsympathetic to the needs of our modern world. The ethics of many of us, including politicians, are being shown to be selfish and shortsighted. We all have our choices, and we all can operate from a soul space. From there, from the power of love, the advice is to trust the overall process and to choose to act from our higher energies in all situations. The power of love, which sparkles with intelligence and is creative, covers all conflicting situations and finds balanced solutions. Basic change stems from individuals.

Natural influences of geographical areas do not alter much, but they are expressed or interpreted in diverse ways, according to the awareness of the people. Nations rise and fall, bringing possibilities into new forms, experimenting with those possibilities, expressing them as they can, and then taking a back seat when other nations with other formulations come to the forefront in the world. Qualities from the same areas may again predominate in a different form at another time. In Italy, for instance, during the Roman Empire great innovative steps in building on the physical level were expressed in architecture and roads, and a thousand years later, during the Renaissance, such innovations were expressed in the arena of the arts and humanities. Some areas of terrain difficult for human habitation still offer basic, primal qualities and energies. In such lands, where humanity has not tempered or refined the energy on physical planes, we have a "gene bank" of vital earth energy. In hot countries, living is easy and offers so little resistance that humankind there finds it difficult to evolve. Great advances in civilization have not generally come from tropical countries, yet wonderful examples of harmonious living have. We are all influenced by geography.

Every society adapts in its unique way, through its culture. Culture is a pattern for our meaning and a gift feeding our creativity. We need the past to establish equilibrium, and the intangible harmony that is our culture is integrated in the changes taking place. Culture, rarely destroyed by change, is integrated and creates new forms in all countries. Each culture has a universal mission, and our individual love is the expression of that mission.

Exercise:

Think of a country you would like to contact more deeply, your own or one that you have visited at some time, one that is familiar in its "feel." I do not try to contact any country whose energies I have not experienced directly, for then I do not have those living energies to contact. My intellect might fool me and have me believe that I know enough about that country to enter it safely, and I don't always trust that part of my mind.

Enter into your highest state of love, and from that state focus on and reach out to the love in the soul of your chosen country. Blend with the qualities there. Listen. Stay harmonized with the energies of the country. Be open for any message. Ask questions if you wish. Trust what you receive while in that high state, knowing that later you can safely act on anything received.

CHAPTER SEVEN

SOULS OF CITIES

I have been dealing with some experiences of relating to the soul level of nature and of countries. Other human groups that have bonded enough to have a unique identity and soul level are cities. We can incorporate traditional angelic forms, like the Christian angels, into our understanding, but we also need to come to a recognition of developments in the angelic world. It is high time we paid attention to the angels of cities, something I found difficult to do, even though our word "civilization" comes from the notion that an advanced society stems from city life. Many aspects of our Western civilization were first developed in the city of Athens, dedicated to Athena, the goddess of wisdom and the arts. To many people cities still seem to offer a better life than does the country, and multitudes continue to stream into the large cities. In them, what we city dwellers gain in easy living and cultural pursuits is balanced by a terrible loss of the natural environment, with its diverse life, stability, and nourishment.

Indeed, my basic perception of cities was of noisy, crowded, smelly, concrete jungles, which I disliked even though I had lived in them most of my life. I could agree with native people, who considered forests to be natural, not wild, and cities to be wild and in need of taming. Oh, I used them. They gave me a job and food and lodging, and their amenities supplied other needs, such as movies, shopping, libraries, theaters, museums, and companionship. I was a city dweller who nevertheless ideologically preferred living outside a city. I thought it would be wonderful to live close to the land, in harmony with all beings, as the Native North American had.

The opportunity arose to fulfill this dream in part when Freya and I left California in 1976 and set off on a lengthy drive across America. Both of us loved the outdoors and chose to sleep in national parks under the stars as much as possible. We wanted to take our time, to stay in places we liked for as long as we liked, and above all to visit and become familiar with Native American areas. I had a particular wish to visit Mesa Verde, for as a child I had fallen in love with pictures of the cliff dwellings I had seen in *A Child's Book of Knowledge*. Visit it we did. We entered by flights of steps built for our modern age. We couldn't have managed the finger- and toe-holds that the Native Americans had used. This was my first disillusionment: those finger- and toe-holds were not created out of harmony with life, but as defense against other Native American tribes. They were built from fear, I concluded. Further disillusionment followed. The rooms were damp, dark with smoke, drafty, too low to stand in, inconveniently far from water, thoroughly uncomfortable, and obviously had been smelly. I realized that in no way would I want to live there. My romantic dreams of dwelling in loving closeness to nature crumbled. A visit to what I considered a slatternly pueblo where Native Americans had been living for hundreds of years confirmed my new opinion. I finally realized that the world had changed, or else I had changed, that I was a citizen of the twentieth century and would be unable to live in such a way without surrendering more than I was willing to.

This was a necessary education for me and freed me to view a city without my previous repugnance. Like others of my culture, I had not considered the possibility that human group constructions have souls, even though I had experienced machine spirits. When I next entered a big city, I wondered if it, too, would have a soul essence. I tuned in and, sure enough, there was a pure overlighting energy, which communicated to me that it was about time I acknowledged that cities also had angels. I was even asked to send it love. That an angel would ask for love melted my heart. Red-faced, I realized that not only had I given cities my hate and dislike, but I had also taken from them and used their vitality without any thanks or helpful return, thus making more difficult their natural task of balancing and blessing the life in their care. It seemed to me that angels of rural and wild areas must have a wonderful time compared with the angels of cities, who have to deal with and try to uplift the most difficult, troubled, and violent areas on the planet.

At the end of that trip across the continent, I settled in a large city, Toronto. Previously I had lived there and had not thought highly of it. Now I began to see beauty as well as advantage, and I joined my local society for improvement of the city. I had no problem living in an eighth-floor apartment in a downtown area. Instead of complaining, I enjoyed it. Somehow the realization that even a city, human-made as it is, has a divine life made all the difference. It changed my attitude, and that changed everything.

When Freya and I began giving workshops in Toronto, one exercise we offered was to attune to the soul of the city. At first people had the same reaction I'd had: "I don't want to attune to a city." "I came to learn more about nature." "There's nothing here worth attuning to." These were a few of the responses. I was adamant, and suggested that there is always something, some tiny thing or place in a city to invest with love. Find that, even if it is a tree, and the love can begin to flow and link you to the angel of the city. We attuned as a group, and even those who felt they had received nothing in the meditation were inspired by the excitement of those who had discovered the creative energy of the city. Of course, everyone encountered different aspects, and all approached from different perspectives, but the differences complemented each other. It was an illuminating exercise for us all and the beginning of a change of attitude for everyone.

Soul and Personality Aspects of Cities

When I gave workshops in Canada and the United States, I would include group attunements to the local city. This was always an interesting and revealing exercise for all of us. Each city had a different energy, and to experience it made the differences more real and vital. When I attuned to a city, I was not so much receiving a message as sensing a pattern of energy and feeling its quality. This, to me, was more direct and real, if less glamorous to others, than a worded message. One day I got a surprise. When I was in Milwaukee for the third time and we were attuning to the soul of the city, in addition to the pure, high energy that I usually experienced I became aware of a beer-drinking burgher type of beingness. I realized that cities not only have a soul essence, but they also have a personality essence, an emotional and mental counterpart, a folk soul. That personality essence is unique, often symbolized to me in an understandable and sometimes funny human form, as in this case of beer-brewing Milwaukee. The form did not always have meaning for me, but it was recognizable to the locals. For example, one impression I had for a particular city was that of a person wearing a bonnet, and I discovered that a certain legendary founder had worn such a bonnet. We sometimes recognize the folk aspect of countries, Uncle Sam, for example. Like humans, cities and countries are not limited to a physical form and a soul. It is enthralling to learn how essence, quality, is manifested at all levels of life.

When I attuned to a city, only sometimes would I become aware of the personality aspect of its energy imaged in a human form, and I never knew when this would happen. Generally the overlighting energy was symbolized as a moving pattern of white light. From the perceptions that came with these experiences I gathered that, as with all life, there are periods of change, introversion and extroversion, creativity, growth, and so on. Now that many beer companies are no longer centered in Milwaukee, perhaps that persona has transformed. I recall that when I visited Buffalo two years running, the angelic energy was on a very different track each time. Perhaps because I am inclined to get into ruts, the angelic world has continually stressed to me the importance of readjustment and the need to have no preconceptions.

Increasingly I realized how our individual consciousness colors whatever we come across and how differently people perceive the same situation. This is especially so when attuning to invisible levels. Although it is an essential part of our humanness to have feelings and emotions, it is also necessary, if we are to function from the pure, deeply felt, and intelligent beauty of our soul selves, that we keep the mirror of our minds and emotions clean. Besides dedication and practice, we need awareness of how expectations form a mold for impressions. On an unconscious level, the imagination, as a vital link to the other worlds, can be glamorized by our very desire to find meaning, quite apart from conscious and unconscious longings and power drives. The path of unfolding is dangerous in intriguing ways. We can be whole, but pay attention!

Soul and Personality Linkage

While attuning again to a particular city with whose higher level and personality energies I was familiar, I was aware that the soul of the city was sending energy, like rain, down to the personality aspect of the city. The personality was absorbing this energy. I realized that this close bond was something very new, and I found it fascinating. While I had reason to believe that the whole planet is changing radically, being filled with new energies, it had not occurred to me that cities were undergoing similar changes. It seemed to be happening in a way very similar to that of humans—a deeper and more sensitive linking with higher or inner levels. Presumably, as more of its inhabitants became more open to higher energies, the closer rapport with the soul level was possible.

Afterward, when attuning to any city, I found it always illuminating to find if the soul and the personality aspects of the city were linked, though I never knew when I would be shown a connection. Actually such a linkage was rare, at least with the cities I visited. I assume that in most cities there are as yet not enough individuals attuned to the soul level to allow for the linkage of the city as a whole. In one place I realized that there was no possibility at that time of a real connection, since the personality of the city was almost antagonistic to the soul area. In another place I had the temerity to suggest to the personality level that it turn to its higher level for greater awareness. That particular personality aspect was independent and wouldn't listen—in fact, it told me to mind my own business. Again I learned that we can't change anyone else, only ourselves.

If, as I see it, there is divine life everywhere in touch with and influencing other divine life, then cities would not be exceptions. People gain a similar awareness in their own unique way; there are as many expressions of truth as there are individuals. I am awed by the ingenuity of God in saying the same thing to me thousands of times without repetition. I admit that sometimes I would like to be able to express myself more scientifically, but I have learned to be content to accept the viewpoints that are mine. I can only be grateful that I no longer hate the thought of living in large cities; I can and do inhabit them with pleasure now. I had been antagonistic to certain topics such as nationalism or politics or cities; now I see them less darkly, even brightly, thanks to the angels who helped me rid myself of limitation.

Relating to Cities

When I returned to my home town, Guelph, I was upset and critical about what had happened to it during my many years' absence. Many beautiful old limestone buildings on the main street had been torn down and replaced by ugly concrete structures. The angel told me not to dwell on the past and to give love and strength to the present city, to relax and feel cleansed. The angelic point of view always returns us to essentials.

Attuning to cities is endlessly interesting to me. In addition to light patterns, I would sometimes get messages from the overlighting angels, and always there was gratitude for any love given them. Naturally, each was unique. In an ancient city in India, for example, the oversoul had a loving attachment to the place, but was so antique that it had little conscious connection with the people. Some angels of cities were very individual, not closely connected with one another and the country. One example is Solo in Java, perhaps because Solo had been a kingdom of its own in recent years and still had a royal family holding on to old patterns. Some angels had deep connections to a previous culture of a place. And others, like the angel of graceful Hangzhou, seemed to want people to come into its influence and go away charmed with it. This particular city appeared to be one of the few places in China where it was advisable to maintain deep links with the past. Some cities, like Bangkok, were so busy with fluctuating energies that there wasn't room for intelligent communication. A more recent contact with the angel of Quito conveyed that its present purpose was incorporation, a blending of various facets, for separateness is a difficulty in the way of functioning properly. Unity is needed and the angel, busy though aware of me and the group with me, was very glad of our conscious move toward the unity in ourselves and in the country. It added that more awareness of its presence and work would also help. Such reminders of angelic awareness cannot but be applicable. Each city had a different relationship with its people. All would like their people to be open to their soul level, for then the angel can pass on seed qualities and energy. And because the intensity of the work of city angels requires great focus, the need for a loving linkage with them is important.

At present I seldom attempt to attune to the souls of cities, for now that I can recognize God everywhere, there does not seem to be a need for specific contact. Many people find the idea of a city soul glamorous and want to know what is going on in their city. That is understandable, but what we see with our eyes, and what our other senses tell us about a city, likewise tells us about its soul. Yet wherever and whatever the city, being open and experiencing it on the soul level gives us a different perspective, which helps minimize the noise, the dirt, the fear, the strangeness, and the often violent behavior of city dwellers. And the wider viewpoint also gives us an impetus to do something about any imbalance.

The cultural process characteristic of an epoch operates most intensely in cities. Since so much of humanity lives in cities and so many of us think of them negatively, it is vital that we clean up our thoughts and dreams of cities and envision them appropriately. The city is our home now, and we need to relate to it as natives in the past related to the earth. We need to change our view of urban and industrial centers, and envision and plan them as suitable and beautiful places to live in now and in the future. The city as it is can awaken our compassion. With sensitivity we can deal with cities, create change in them, and build them for the future. In cities we can find balance and joy. The mystery of God is alive there.

Exercise:

Attune within to the highest that you know, to your own spiritual space. In the joy of that realm, link to the similar ranges of the soul of a city you know and wish to contact. Relax in the qualities. Open yourself to the intelligence of the city and listen. Put into form what is being communicated to you. Take time, for a city is a complex being. You can trust what you receive when you are in your "highest" state, and you can later safely act on what is revealed, if necessary.

⌘ CHAPTER EIGHT

Psychic Dimensions

At this time of planetary change, so many developments are emerging that we have difficulty keeping up with them. Various cultures are converging, presenting us with different viewpoints on old patterns. Technologies, particularly the computer, are changing our life-styles, and other dimensions are making themselves known in a new way. Science has accepted paradox in acknowledging that light is both a wave and a particle, and it is being accepted that our invisible thoughts and emotions have physical effects.

We deal with many dimensions in ourselves and how they interact, common classifications of them being body, heart, mind, and soul, or the physical, emotional, intellectual, and spiritual. Firm boundaries keep disappearing as our information expands. Realizing that our air is full of invisible radio and television waves can help us accept that there is more on this Earth than has been dreamed of. We have out-of-the-world experiences in waking consciousness or in dreams. Most cultures have accepted otherworld wisdom through divination, oracles, shamans, or channelers. There are dimensions of the inner worlds to be explored and to attract an adventurous person. All these areas may be perplexing, and often we confuse them—as, for example, by thinking that because we see something invisible like an aura, we are spiritual. But being human and having inquiring minds, we want to understand!

In my own life, the first important experience that was out of the ordinary was, as I have related, the gigantic, awesome, and expanding experience that God was within, followed by an increasing knowledge that I have—that everyone and everything has—a beautiful and loving core that I can consciously contact and draw close to. The contact led me to relate to a similar core in other life. I found that human groupings have unique identities and separate souls. Such unique groups have life energy on the highest level, for everything is of God, but they also have personality levels arising from the thoughts and feelings of that group. I first noticed this level when contacting cities and found an emotional and intellectual aspect arising from its people, often conveyed to me through a picturesque human costume.

I am calling these other-dimensional aspects of human groupings the psychic or astral world. This level is made up of our emotional and mental creations, including past human feelings and thoughts and those of humans still connected to Earth after death. As I see it, we humans have emotional and mental bodies for expressing individual emotional and intellectual energies, and they also come together in the psychic dimension to form a collective entity. These entities are powerful, especially the emotional ones.

Power of the Psychic World

Consider fear. We humans know it. In a collective grouping such as a city, the presence of fear can be identified with a particular area, and people coming into that area may suddenly experience fear, to their surprise, as I did when driving through a certain area of Chicago. As a human being, I resonate to all emotions, and as long as I am responsive to fear, I will experience it where it is expressed. Because human fears are continually being expressed and added to, we create a planetary entity of fear. On the higher levels there is the seed quality of that energy, including positive and negative, courage and fear. Since we have been expressing a great deal of fear on the planet, the resulting energy is greatly out of balance and has often been called "devil." From the angelic perspective, all qualities have their places and functions, but because we are not aware of how our psychic expressions give creative power to this polarization of one aspect of a universal quality, we see only the separation. We do not realize that we are creating these fears and that we can change them and bring them back to their original wholeness.

Similarly, our thoughts have created entities at the psychic level. In the West, so often have people thought of Santa Claus, by various names, that a definite image of Santa has gained a reality that influences us. So often have people thought of or painted a gentle Jesus, meek and mild, and often blue-eyed and fair haired, that the image predominates in our culture. Shakespeare's play *The Tragedy of King Richard III* pictures a villainous English king, which was the image that the victorious Tudors gave of the last Plantagenet. Actually, Richard III is said to have been one of the finest kings that country ever had, but this enemy version is the one we encounter in the thought world.

We meet these inner psychic dimensions in our lives, consciously or unconsciously. They are part of what we deal with, forces that we express and empower. They are our own personality aspects as well as being separate created entities. We are always contributing our thoughts and feelings, building up the content of the psychic world. Often we glamorize sensory images of them, especially if someone "sees" them visually. We even relegate these images to a spiritual dimension. What is important is that we can consciously interact with and affect psychic entities, especially when we relate to them with love. We can be of help to them.

I had a disconcerting example of being influenced by another dimension in Hawaii in 1986. There I attuned to Pelé, goddess of Hawaii's volcanoes. To me she was very tied to fire and the creative principle. On the island of Hawaii the general belief was that bad luck would follow anyone who took away any pieces of Pelé's lava. I and my friends found the glistening lava irresistibly tempting, and we gathered and secreted bits of the volcanic rock in our baggage, which is an illegal act. I myself am not superstitious, and anyway I believed egotistically that I had an "in" with Pelé because I had attuned to her. On my arrival home I had my first automobile accident. Then I got a cold, which I never do, and other things started to go wrong. I remembered Pelé's "curse," wrapped up my lava, and mailed it back to Hawaii. Evidently, every year the Hawaii Volcanoes National Park receives hundreds to thousands of packages of rocks and other volcanic products, along with letters describing the bad luck that had plagued the senders since they picked up these souvenirs in Hawaii.

I don't believe that curses have power or that spirit metes out punishment. What I do believe is that there are powers on psychic levels that we would do well to recognize for what they are: qualities polarized negatively in emotions like fear or positively in emotions like gaiety. We have all experienced the contagion of both laughter and fear. We often emphasize the negative more than the positive, as exemplified in our newspaper headlines. When we recognize that the news is almost always negative and presents an unbalanced view, we can accept it as only part of the truth and seek the whole truth.

We come under the influence of the negative, of stories in the news or of "ghoulies and ghosties," as long as we resonate to them. We are free of their influence when we no longer give them power over us and instead honor the balance of love. This is the capacity of humans; it is our task to adjust the polarization. Our makeup includes all possibilities, and if anything remains in us that continues to act in separation from the whole—and none of us is perfect—we may react to a so-called superstition. In my encounter with the lava, I realized I had been insensitive and had felt superior to the beliefs of another culture; I had broken their laws. Thus I drew a pattern to myself. I apologized, for recognizing our limited outlook and taking it into love helps heal the incident. And I learned that it is wise to honor all beliefs, all gods, for we have given them much power. There is truth behind superstitions and old wives' tales. The same lesson is there: love. Become so loving that, as the Bible puts it, Satan finds nothing in us.

Connected with Old Energies

During this visit I had a most interesting interaction with an inner reality at an ancient temple ruin. Realizing that gods are energy force fields, archetypes, qualities that we have personified on the psychic level and given names and recognition, even worship, I tuned in to the energies of the old Hawaiian gods there. I found them functioning only on the psychic, or personality, level,—a sorry lot, like pale ghosts. They knew they were passé and neglected, and were very dejected about it. They were wandering around in a twilight, feeling lost. As I discovered later, in 1819 they had been suddenly abandoned or banished by decree of the Hawaiian king in attempts to meet the modern world. This decree had been urged by women and supported by the fact that Europeans who ignored the taboos of the island religion came to no harm.

I realized that these phantoms did not have to continue in their limbo. Like us humans, they had lost conscious contact with their core. They, too, could identify with what they really were, the qualities out of which creation arises. So I talked to them, told them they could claim their true essence, and sent them love. Over time it seemed to me that eventually most of them understood and chose to identify with their shining selves.

But one, a god of war, remained dejected. Having had a lot of practice in my workshops in attuning to the quality of courage, the basic quality of a warrior, I tried to love this presence into transformation by conveying an ideal of warring for the weak. It didn't change. Finally, it said that it would have to get used to the idea and asked me to return later. I returned to it at various times, and gradually it became strong and shining. It was a very moving experience for me to attune to it at that time. At the end of my visit, it was almost wholly identified with its real self. I read later that when King Kamehameha II broke the *kapu* system (prohibitions in the Polynesian religion, from which we derive our word "taboo"), he had kept one warrior god!

When I visited Hawaii several years later, I found these old gods still consciously linked with their higher energies. I do not think they will ever again become limited to their previous god personality, though as long as there is human memory or identity attached to them, they will have a certain life on the psychic level. I suppose they could be revived, but perspectives have changed so much that some old forms are no longer of much use in Hawaii or Greece or elsewhere. In other days, we called on the gods and felt close to their qualities. In Greece the gods lived on Mount Olympus, and people mingled with them. Today we recognize that gods and people are mingling within each individual as we resonate with angelic qualities in manifestion. It is said that Greece's decline began when its gods were relegated to planets and outer space, instead of staying on Mount Olympus, where gods and humans were once close.

The qualities the gods personified are still with us, now more commonly recognized as archetypal forces working in individuals. Some negative expressions, like terrorism, violence, and other "evils," seem to be manifest as *never* before. There is, in general, more consent and more opportunity for fulfillment of conscious and unconscious desires as authoritarian customs and regimes are being abolished. People are attuning to and living out a greater range of the pairs of opposites, and hence have less need of outer gods to lean on. In this greater attunement, we can resonate with and understand the qualities better. The old gods, unless separated from their own reality, rejoice in their own demise and themselves find a closer identity to their source qualities. In Hawaii there has been a belief arising among schoolchildren of all races in ghostly Night Walkers who kill humans. This belief is based on stories of the ancient Hawaiian guards of the old nobles, the Alii, and it has created fear in the children. I felt that the old gods were working to negate that revived cultural superstition.

Clearing Old and New Patterns

The past or present fate of the old gods may not mean much in our Western society, but the cleansing and balancing of our own selves and our problems is paralleled by the expurgation of the shadows of the old gods. In our cultures we may have done away with demons, with ancient negativities named by us, but the psychic factors that breed them, such as fear and prejudice, are as actively at work as ever. They are a pollution in our psychic atmosphere, a psychic violence as real and more ancient than outer pollution, and it is a wonderful thought that we can help clear that atmosphere by our loving concern. Our upset planet urgently needs all the help it can get, and we cannot overrate the influence of our present emotional creations in building up modern demons. We may not call them demons, but the fear stalking city streets is a powerful influence. The increasing number of counselors dealing with personal problems is an indication of a tremendous surfacing of old repressions and hurts, a clearing away of shadows. As we each purge our own private anguish, our own demons, we can help the whole more. It is a time of planetary cleansing.

The surfacing of old patterns of enmity in various places, like the ethnic warfare in the Balkans, is but another example of the problems that need to be addressed. We as a civilization are at least beginning to see that certain human actions are no longer permissible, though we search for a way to act on our conclusions. We often forget that we have patterns of enmity in North America, such as our own ethnic cleansing of the Native Americans or our treatment of African-Americans, and thus also have a responsibility to help in any separation from unity. As we claim our greater awareness, we help with our love.

There are, of course, many living peoples who are still supporting old patterns. Most of us still subscribe to old guilt patterns, such as the idea of being born in sin. We can learn from old stories and traditions, as psychology is doing, to help us deal with our own personality shadows; our psychic atmosphere is easier to breathe without these bogeys. As humans, we have all qualities, all archetypes, within us, and when we come across situations corresponding to a particular archetype, the equivalent myth can be activated. We can grow by resonating to the qualities, exploring them, accepting them, and loving them. Then our awareness expands.

For our own learning, there are fascinating studies and stories contained in ancient places all over the world. Stones still speak of their history, through the energy they contain. As an example, I have attuned to the Clava Cairns, one of the many prehistoric stone circles and burial chambers in Scotland, and felt an energy present, turned not toward the stones but toward the Sun. I wondered why life is still there and was told that the physical uniqueness of the circle still has power. It seemed to me that the builders and users of that locale, though they lived a hard life, accepted their lot instead of resisting it and therefore were joyful and genuinely turned to the spiritual, even in their death ceremonies.

Old Connection to the Whole

An exotic example of one of many ways for connecting to the loving intelligence of the planet was shown to me in Nepal. There the Kumari, the Living Goddess, is honored. She is chosen at a young age, must come from a Buddhist family, must have certain traditional Buddhist marks of excellence, must have never bled, must have no physical imperfection, and is severely tested for fearlessness. Once selected, she is installed in her own ancient and beautifully carved residence temple in Katmandu (there are other Kumaris elsewhere) and is watched constantly to ensure that she has no accidents that might draw blood, not even a pinprick. Normal education and play are thought to be inappropriate for her, since she is considered to be a goddess. She leaves her residence only once a year, when she is paraded through the streets of Katmandu and the Hindu king of Nepal pays obeisance to her. She is also watched for certain gestures that have traditional meaning for the country.

A Kumari evidently once foretold trouble in the following year for a reigning king, and he did die that year. When her menstrual blood starts to flow, that is the end of her divinity; the goddess has left and another child has to be found.

Hindus are allowed into her temple, and for non-Hindus she will appear briefly on a balcony for an unphotographed viewing; there I saw her twice. Ex-Kumaris have a hard life after such a limited and sheltered upbringing, with no training for domesticity or wifehood, and they also suffer because it is considered unlucky for any man to marry one. The present Kumari, I gather, is being given some education and a few friends to help her overcome some of these disabilities. A Nepalese friend of mine interviewed an ex-Kumari, and I found it intriguing that she had no memory of the occasions when she made the special gestures that had meaning for the priests, perhaps foretelling the future or indicating action to be taken. It does seem that at those times she was taken over by a supranormal energy, perhaps in a way similar to the trances of the Delphic Oracles of Greece. When I attuned to the Kumari energy, it appeared to me as very beautiful and compassionate. I asked if it had not outlived its time, and it answered, "*Not yet; I am still of service to the country, though I foresee an end. I can only hope that my energy will still have an outlet in the future.*" When I asked for a suggestion about a future form, I was told that events were too much in flux for any foresight.

Recently I went for a walk with a friend and her three little girls, one of whom was very full of good spirits and was thoroughly enjoying herself, until she pricked her finger on a thorn and produced a drop of blood. Her demeanor changed completely, and from then on she was quiet and withdrawn. Her mother mentioned that this was remarkable. It reminded me of the Kumari story; drawn blood certainly dissipated power for that little girl.

Most cultures have examples of phenomenal happenings, like people entering trance states and speaking with a different voice, or reading minds from a distance, or channeling, which is common today. All these are different ways of approaching the intelligence of the universe, in ourselves and in unseen dimensions, whether human or angelic. They can be helpful or otherwise, according to how we understand and use them. I myself like to know about and learn from them, to see if they have relevance. In countries with ancient cultures, I continued to come across energies that had been personified as gods, and my understanding of them as the personification of essences of quality seemed to be confirmed. For instance, connected with the Great Wall of China was a great compassionate protection, wielding a hidden benign influence on both sides of the wall, yet appearing as fierce Mongolian-like beings on the personality level. It was a shadow of its old self, yet it remained to keep a benevolent eye on this barrier. On the psychic level, blood was flowing from the foundations. I asked if this was wasted blood and was told that it was not, that it had been necessary for the times and for the good of the whole. It welcomed foreigners, with the idea that our visits could promote world unity.

Old Energies Changing

At Chiang Mai in Thailand in 1989, before visiting a nearby tribe, I became aware of an angel of the hill tribes in an area that included Thailand, Laos, and Burma. From a lower personality level it gave the impression of fierceness of color, with sharp pointy fingers, quickly moving; on a higher level, it seemed wraithlike, disappearing like mist. I asked why it was disappearing, and it replied that the energies that formed the tribes, the individual strong cultures, did not fit into the interconnectedness that is emerging in the world. Although tourists demand tribal artwork, thus encouraging their existence as tribes, and even though tribal identities seem strong and separate, more so than North American Indian tribes, the distinctions are vanishing. When I commiserated with the angels on this, believing the world would be poorer with the loss of such unique and colorful cultures, the angel replied that their cultural artifacts, such as the brilliant woven bands, had already been appreciated and adopted elsewhere, thus passing into the planetary whole. When I still felt sad about the variety that would be lost, the reply came that variety would not be lost; what would be lost was some savagery. Competiveness could be expressed more appropriately in a transformed creativity, more like winning a game for joy instead of for separate, polarized, and opposing factions. I pointed out that all over the world events had taken a different turn, that separate nationalities were insisting on being themselves. The angel of the hill tribes reminded me that most other groupings were seeking a unity they had lost, while the hill tribes had not lost their identity; they had never been united and were small migrant units that could no longer support themselves. Their creativity was played out; one could say that they had been successful and now needed to change. The angel did not know what new birth would bring for these tribes, but when different cultures come together, new forms appear.

The Flow of Energies

I call these energies "old gods" and have given examples from older cultures. But energies of the angelic world and our representation of them will always exist in the wholeness of the planet. Our human understanding of them changes with the times, and new ones appear with new human creations. Immemorial nature energies, the angel messengers of God in nature, continue. Whenever a human group fashions a unique identity, there is a counterpart on inner levels. This is true for families, businesses, schools, cities, countries, and so on. Always the energies flow and change. In China, when attuning to a silk industry spirit, I found it glad that increasingly modern technology was making obsolete the repetitive labor necessary in the past. This being seemed to understand the human heart as few others do, perhaps because the means used to produce silk material is sometimes to be deplored, even though the end product is very beautiful. The spirit reminded me that the aim for humanity is to be as free as the angels, but with more initiative and creativity, and that this idea is new for China and would necessitate a tremendous break with tradition. But China can contribute a subtle feel for the togetherness of things, a sensitive awareness of human workings—to me the sort of sensitivity that in the past has been expressed in their delicate and beautiful artwork, picking out basics from the plethora of nature to create pattern.

The old gods still have power in the psychic realms, as exemplified by the tremendous public response to the Findhorn nature contact. An undefined part of people yearns for fairies or angels, arousing a longing for a beauty that has been lost in our present civilization. The very name of the Gaia hypothesis (the hypothesis that the world is a self-regulating system) also draws a surprisingly wide reaction from nonscientific folk. The modern oversouls of countries and cities, which I have described, as well as the oversouls of families, of industries, of houses, and so on, are not generally recognized. We perceive certain family traits or other forms of uniqueness, like the certain type of clothing that distinguishes IBM personnel (and such icons keep changing), but our present culture rarely links with higher energies. We have forgotten that life is a continuum and that nothing can exist on only the physical level; everything has counterparts on all levels of being. There is no energy in existence that is not ensouled by some kind of living intelligence. An empty house may be an empty house, but it still carries the imprint of the architect and the builders. If it has been lived in, it gains an atmosphere from the thoughts and emotions of its inhabitants. It has a counterpart on other levels deriving from a combination of the soul and personality essence of the architect, the materials, the builders, the inhabitants, and the visitors. Powerful events leave their mark in it. We often recognize uniqueness on a feeling level; some houses are said to be haunted, which could indicate a personality power, whereas Mary chapels in old churches often have a wonderful pure feeling, an angelic force.

In our busy modern world, our current creations, our omnipresent machines, are very closely tied to the attitudes and motives of the builders and users, for the essence of machines is part of a human subset, the result of the creativity gifted to us as humans. We take the substance of the physical world and reform physical matter according to our mental designs, unconsciously imbuing the designs with our emotions, and then we use the products. Our creation is not usually the pure, free-ranging angelic substance of natural things, even though it is connected with, say, the angel of the metal of which it is composed. Its strength on the essence level is as strong or as weak as the quality of the human attitudes attached to it. When I first contacted a machine spirit, which took me some time because I am not a lover of the straight-line, colorless appearance of machinery, I remember I called it "black," my way of distinguishing it from a nature deva. We can blend almost completely with our tools, our machines: I knew a motorcycle rider who so melded with his machine that it was part of him. When we can do this with our own machines, our computers, say, and make them instruments of our love, machinery can be a great force for betterment. The spiritual energy of human technologies and activities, as a subset of the human and as our responsibility, is of benefit to the planet when we act from our own wholeness. The planet shows an emphatic lack of that wholeness at present! To put it another way, we humans focus our creation at the mental and psychic levels, often with narrow or selfish motives and without taking the larger picture into account, and therefore we construct in limitation, incompletely. I try to remind myself to make my computer more complete by adorning it with a delightful wooden Buddha, images of loved animals, or other symbols of broader energies. Technology has a definite part to play in our unfolding, and, according to our awareness, we make it a tool for good or for ill.

Our culture creates its modern icons, such as Superman or Mr. Spock. We can also make the idea of a god ludicrous nowadays with such concepts as gods or devas of human artifacts like spoons—I have seen kitchen drawers labeled "Spoon Devas"—although having spoons as a reminder of the spiritual is a great notion. The essence energy of items such as spoons is tied to humanity and has a generic and intelligent core linked with human creativity; without humans, the energy would not exist. Yet the limiting line between human subsets and free angels is a fine one, and I had a wonderful example of this in 1989. Here in the United States a friend of mine, with his young son, visited a McDonald's restaurant, and became aware of a beautiful angel of the species McDonald. The angel had an excited sense of a new awakening, of an expanded life touching global dimensions. It conveyed that there would be changes in the company's procedures, and shortly afterward McDonald's did announce some environmentally inclusive policies. My friend also felt that a contribution to the angel's enlivenment was the joy expressed at a new branch in Moscow. There the company's training of its waiters to be helpful and to smile was exceptional, even unprecedented, and joyfully surprised people. The delight of Muscovites in being able to get lots of food of a different kind, even if they had to wait in line for ages, had also helped create joy. I understand that when any group, or any human, allows higher, service-oriented, ideal energies to be expressed, they can be said, at least at that moment, to have gained angelic status! This tale helped me to realize again how powerful and creative our human expressions of angelic qualities can be.

I believe that the time taken for the generation of soul uniqueness in a human group depends on the bonding capacity of the group. If the group is truly functioning with pure energies in service, it has angelic status. Or it may be that an angel, in some divine plan, comes first and draws people to it. Recognizing such a possibility, and giving it the energy of love, helps the process of its birth. I was first aware of an angel of a human group at Findhorn, as I have explained in more detail in *To Hear the Angels Sing*, and I have already referred to the soul level of cities and countries.

Accepting our Lineages

The biblical saying that the sins of the fathers extend to the third and fourth generations is to me another way of recognizing group identity, in this context in the family or clan unconscious. I think it is no accident that we are born in a certain family, for there are relationships and situations to be worked out in them. I was made extraordinarily aware of family resemblances when I returned to Canada after an absence of thirty years and met with old friends. I found, to my amusement and dismay, that my friends were strikingly like my memories of their parents. They were about the same age as their parents had been when I last saw them; they talked like them, had comparable mannerisms, and even thought similarly. I was told that I was a mixture of both my parents! I believe part of coming to terms with our past and our family soul is to recognize and accept our backgrounds without judgment or condemnation, for then we cease reacting and no longer generate counterproductive energies. As we restructure our individual reactions and break patterns, we can be the means of completing a family karma. We often need help recognizing our reactions, enriching the field of psychological and psychiatric counseling. Always, it is important to find a balance into which love can enter.

Interaction between us and the subtle energies of other levels is always present, and we cannot escape absorbing their atmosphere any more than we can escape breathing in the air. At this time of planetary change I see the angels, the essence of the gods, the elements, the Christ, immersing the Earth more strongly with power, drawing out of us our angelic qualities. If we resist their help, we generally suffer until we change. This is a work of transformation, of extending our awareness. This strong energizing of the planet affects us in many ways, and we react both positively and negatively. For instance, I can see the revival of nationalism as a seeking for a necessary identity or as a falling back into outworn patterns. We have to discover how to learn from and balance the new potencies. Meeting with new energies gives us the opportunity to grow and change.

These energies bring opportunities for a state of consciousness in which we can participate more fully with the planet as a whole. They aid transformation on all levels. All energy moves through a form of consciousness. Consciousness is the link between God and humans, the balance between spirit and matter. Some have called it the universal body of Christ. Angels or energies have compassion for our difficulties in accepting new consciousness, new boundaries, new coherence. And our difficulties can be vast, for it may seem that we lose ourselves, lose at least our egos, if we enter their dimensions. Our cultures give us no training for these connections, though the heart of most religions does.

In many areas we have polluted both our physical and psychic air; and we have to address both issues. We need to be clear about how we are functioning, realizing that spirit, love, is the power in all facets of life. I believe we should acknowledge and work consciously with the invisible levels as we encounter them; they are part of the planet and part of our own human creation, particularly on emotional levels. It has been my experience that as we invoke the highest that we know, our inner core, and from there love our world and even ourselves, we change both our world and ourselves. Firmly centered in love, we are safe from unpleasant psychic influences, and we can transform them. As human beings, we have been allowed to contact consciously our inner/outer divinity in all forms, to learn from emotional, mental, and physical environments, and to metamorphose.

Change is manifesting in ways new to us, and increasing our awareness. Certainly, our pollution of the Earth is making us sensitive to our links with the planet. Many so-called negativities are awakening us, forcing us to look at life differently. There is renewed and continuing interest in archetypes and in the qualities of the female energy, of goddesses, which have suffered from neglect. All of this inner work leads to a greater understanding and recognition of the love that is the basis of energy. The power of love continues to astonish. It is the answer to individual and planetary problems.

Exercise

Have you ever had an inexplicable experience, positive or negative, about which you would like some understanding? If so, rise to your highest self and put the situation into the arms of love, of God. This gives you an opportunity to see everything from a different perspective. A problem seen from the viewpoint of wholeness often disappears or changes completely.

Or you may come across a geographical place, say one with the remains of a previous civilization, that beckons you. Attune to the highest level within and listen. When I do that, I may get the feel of those who have lived there, not information per se but a feeling that gives me perspective. If a contact is made, know that there is still life there, life that you can always help by sending love.

I am often asked about attuning to another person. I don't do such a thing without permission, because I respect the individuality and integrity of others. Of course, we can always send loving energy to others and pray for them, without judgment or expectation. We can pray for the highest good of another; for sick people, the highest good may very well be that they die and experience new beginnings.

CHAPTER NINE

IN PRAISE OF LOVE

Having expounded on various issues in which love has been the transforming agent, I would now like to underline certain conclusions. Our Western culture has so emphasized the material world with its wonderful secrets and discoveries that the spiritual world, and particularly its divine core, has until recently been shunned as unreal, unscientific, or, at best, so distant and foreign that it is out of our reach. In fact, God is closer than breathing, nearer than hands and feet. It is within us, giving us life at all times. It is the life force in all of life, a loving energy that is forever becoming more aware of itself. It is the most powerful force in the universe.

The world is seething with love, expressing love through nature and its beauty, and longing to be conscious in us. Humanity has been gifted with magnificent vehicles of expression in the physical, emotional, mental, and spiritual realms. We seek in many directions and in many dimensions, and we will continue to seek until we find that pearl of great price within. When we do finally become aware of it, generally through suffering and trial and error, we are led, in whatever way is best for us, the way dearest to us, with love to greater love.

In an increasingly difficult and violent world, accepting that the answer to our problems is love may seem a faulty conclusion, ridiculous or impossible to achieve. We think in the short term, believing that one life is all we have. It is ridiculous to limit our existence to one chance only and to believe we are snuffed out or relegated to heaven or hell after a period of some seventy years on the Earth. It is ridiculous to deny that love would not give us endless opportunities to be what we are: beloved offshoots of that love. We are loved, but in the cultural climate of our times, and in our imbalance, we have lost ourselves. Lost as we are, we are still given every chance to find ourselves. This planet has been called the school of hard knocks, and every one of those knocks is designed, in an intelligent, aware universe, to point us in the direction of love. We fight and suffer, and the more we resist, the more difficult we make it for ourselves. When we accept and step out of what has been holding us to our limited patterns, we become free to love ourselves and our world.

We learn through our choices. We have been given freedom to choose, and we have used that gift to the fullest, to an extreme where our individual freedoms are threatening us. Our polluted planet tells us that we have gone too far on the path of individuality, that we are linked with the planet and with each other in ways we have not considered until now. It is telling us the old story that we have spurned: that we need to love each other and all aspects of life, or we will not be able to continue to live in our world. The Earth may be shouting "Doomsday" at us, but we now know that we have created that doomsday. We can choose to change. We have that freedom, unlike the Alaskan bear and other life forms I have contacted. We learn to make changes through judging our good and bad actions, until we realize that "goods" and "bads" are our own projections and that everything works together. Then our choices become individually part of the whole.

We have dominion over the planet, and we have taken on that dominion disastrously because we have not yet accepted responsibility for the whole. As stewards, we have many choices and decisions to make and to follow through. We can notice if plants or wayside trees are yellow and need care; we can decide whether or not to use fertilizers that poison other life. Change is coming about so quickly that the natural world does not have time to adapt. Are we not accountable for its continuing existence? We have poured concrete over thousands of acres of land, preventing natural growth. Can we, through our love, bring this concrete more into the wholeness of life? And are there choices to be made in our use of the motor car and in our use of nuclear energy? We must become accountable for our actions.

We cannot go on usurping the resources of the world for our own comfort without taking responsibility for other life and other humans. American pioneers pushed west to make more and more farms out of forests and prairies. Now there is little forest or prairie for farms, and the farmlands themselves are being used for dwelling places. We have used the Earth without thought or thanks. Can changes be brought about with greater awareness of the whole? At present we use all possible resources, whether physical, emotional, or mental, for the benefit of our health. Perhaps we can realize unimagined states of health, accept death as natural, and flow more graciously with the changes of life.

As we love more, we honor more: we honor pain, we honor beauty, we honor all paths, we honor each other. We begin to glimpse the wonder of life in its infinite forms, and the wonder that is within us. Through the ages humanity has given wonderful proof of its spirit in selfless acts, in creating beautiful works of art, in plain kindness. We can continue in this spirit and choose to love, let love steep our being. We can enhance our world. We are being asked to do that right now.

Love is the basis of intelligence. Both intelligence and love are part of our world, but love is the deeper of the two. Intelligence, although it is part of love, is our instrument of awareness. For awareness, for creation, there needs to be separation; the one has to become the many. True intelligence ensures that love is expressed in the way best for all, and love continues to invoke and sustain intelligence and eventually draws all back together. Without the vast yearning power of love, there would be no reaching out, no questioning, no desire for answers. Without love, intelligence at the human level can be an instrument to power, for without love, intelligence is liable to be used for solitary and self-seeking pursuits, confined to the intellect. Mental conclusions, the naming of things, are impersonal and powerless unless we give them meaning or power by the energy of our feelings, by our reactions and projections. To see with the mind of love is to see without blinkers. The intellect is a focusing instrument, and rightly so. The intellect can know that it is part of the whole, but it is not enough to know intellectually; it is necessary to reach out to others, to experience being part of the whole. Love makes that bridge, brings the feeling of belonging, of being at one. When harnessed to love, the mind is open to shafts of light from other areas. They come as ideas, feelings, or intuitions from the whole network of life of which we are a part but from which we are normally isolated. From our senses we learn to progress through life to greater enlightenment. Love always adds other dimensions. Besides, it makes us feel good, and life should be joyful. Then we do not erect fences against our conditions and so can flow with events.

Resistance stops the flux of energies around us as well as giving pain. When we stop resisting, love can enter, life can enter.

Whatever life brings us is an agent of love, although at the time it may seem to bring the opposite. We can focus with love by not always giving ourselves over to the sheer joy of its wonderful feeling, and instead concentrating, listening to what is there. Attention to the energies around and within is sharpened.

We create with love, with passion. Love intensifies and enlarges, bringing greater accuracy to whatever it is focused on. It is not wishful thinking, although we can get confused about that. Love seeks truth, and when we are dedicated to truth, we see truth. It is in our nature to want to know truth for ourselves, and through honesty we recognize it. Seeking, we will find. Love changes everything. We can look at an ugly boot with love, and it becomes beautiful. We can look at violence and become compassionate, perhaps compassionate enough to do something. If we look at ourselves with love, what a relief! We can glory in the attitude of being pliant to softness; it has taken aeons for life to become more and more sensitive, to honor the delicate. Now we can love.

We may think that this love is too difficult. But love is a simple thing, so simple it gets passed over. We all know about it. What is our favorite color, movie, or breed of dog? These are the ordinary things that we love. There are people we love, things we love doing. Wherever we are, we can find some little thing to love, and start the flow of love within. It is in everyday life that love is needed most. It is up to each one of us to love, to become what we truly are. As a consequence, we will find ourselves fulfilled and the planet saved.

BIBLIOGRAPHY

Abraham, Kurt. *Balancing the Pairs of Opposites.* White City, Ore.: Lampus Press, 1993.

Arroyo, Stephen. *Astrology, Psychology and the Four Elements: An Energy Approach to Astrology and Its Use in the Counseling Arts.* Davis, Calif.: CRCS Publications, 1975.

Augros, Robert M. and George N. Stanciu. *The New Story of Science.* Chicago: Gateway Editions, 1984.

Bailey, Alice. *The Destiny of Nations.* New York: Lucis Trust, 1949.

Berman, Morris. *Coming to Our Senses: Body and Spirit in the Hidden History of the West.* New York: Bantam New Age Book, 1989.

Berry, Thomas. *The Dream of the Earth.* San Francisco: Sierra Club Books, 1988.

Berton, Pierre. *Why We Act Like Canadians.* Toronto: McClelland & Stewart, 1982.

Bohm, David. *Wholeness and the Implicate Order.* London: Routledge & Kegan Paul, 1981.

Campbell, Joseph. *The Hero's Journey: Joseph Campbell on His Life and World.* Edited by Phil Coustineau. San Francisco: Harper & Row, 1990.

————— *Myths to Live By.* New York: Bantam Books, 1972.

—————*The Power of Myth.* With Bill Moyers. New York: Doubleday, 1988.

Chopra, Deepak. *Quantum Healing.* New York: Bantam New Age Book, 1989.

————— *Ageless Body, Timeless Mind.* New York: Harmony Books, 1993.

Cobb, Noel. *Archetypal Imagination: Glimpses of the Gods in Life and Art.* Hudson, N. Y.: Lindisfarne Press, 1992.

Dossey, Larry. *Recovering the Soul: A Scientific and Spiritual Search.* New York: Bantam Books, 1989.

Dubos, René. *The Wooing of the Earth.* New York: Charles Scribner's Sons, 1980.

———— *So Human an Animal.* New York: Charles Scribner's Sons, 1968.

Emmons, Michael L. *The Inner Source: A Guide to Meditative Therapy.* Impact Publishers, 1978.

Feininger, Andres. *Trees.* Viking Press, 1968.

Greene, Liz. *Saturn: A New Look at an Old Devil.* New York: Samuel Weiser Inc., 1976.

Grof, Stanislav. *The Adventure of Self Discovery: Dimensions of Consciousness and New Perspectives in Psychotherapy and Inner Exploration.* State University of New York Press, 1988.

Harmon, Willis. *Global Mind Change.* Indianapolis: Knowledge Systems, 1988.

Hastings, Arthur. *With the Tongues of Men and Angels: A Study of Channeling.* Orlando: Holt Rinehart and Winston Inc., 1991.

Hillman, James. *The Thought of the Heart & the Soul of the World.* Dallas: Spring Publications, 1995.

Houston, Jean. *The Search for the Beloved: Journey into Sacred Psychology.* Los Angeles: Jeremy P. Tarcher Inc., 1987.

Joy, Brugh. *Avalanche: Heretical Reflections on the Dark and the Light.* New York: Balantine Books, 1990.

Jung, Carl. *Civilization in Transition.* Vol. 10 of Bolingen Series XX, Princeton: Princeton University Press, 1964.

Krishnamurti, J. *Freedom from the Known.* New York: Harper & Row, 1969.

Landau, Rom, *God Is My Adventure.* New York: Alfred A. Knopf, 1936.

Lee, Jung Young. *The Theology of Change: A Christian Concept of God in an Eastern Perspective.* New York: Orbis Books, 1979.

Leichtman, Robert R. & Carl Japikse. "Tuning into Divine Archetypes." *Magical Blend,* no. 18 (Feb/Apr. 1988).

Lemesurier, Peter. *This New Age Business.* Forres: Findhorn Press, 1990.

Maclean, Dorothy. *The Soul of Canada: An Overview of National Identity.* Lorian Press, 1977.

———— *To Hear the Angels Sing.* Hudson, N.Y: Lindisfarne Press, 1980.

Matthews, Caitlin & John. *The Western Way: A Practical Guide on the Western Mystery Tradition.* London: Arkana, 1985.

McGoldrick, Monica, John K. Pearce and Joseph Giordano. *Ethnicity and Family Therapy.* New York: Guildford Press, 1982.

Moore, Thomas. *Care of the Soul.* New York: HarperCollins, 1992.

———— *Soul Mates.* New York: HarperCollins, 1994.

Nicholson, Shirley, and Brenda Rosen, compilers. *Gaia's Hidden Life: The Unseen Intelligence of Nature.* Wheaton, Ill.: Quest Books, 1990.

Parisen, Maria. *Angels and Mortals: Their Co-Creative Power.* Wheaton, Ill.: Quest Books, 1990.

Perry, John Weir. *The Heart of History: Individuality in Evolution.* State University of New York Press, 1987.

Powe, B. W. *A Canada of Light.* Toronto: Somerville House, 1997.

Sardello, Robert. *Facing the World with Soul: The Reimagination of Modern Life.* Hudson, N.Y.: Lindisfarne Press, 1992.

Sheldrake, Rupert. *The Rebirth of Nature: The Greening of Science and God.* New York: Bantam Books, 1991.

Spangler, David. *Reflections on the Christ.* Findhorn Lecture Series, 1978.

———— *Everyday Miracles: The inner Art of Manifestation.* New York: Bantam Books, 1996.

———— *A Pilgrim in Aquarius.* Forres: Findhorn Press, 1996.

———— & William Irwin Thompson. *Reimagination of the World.* Santa Fe: Bear & Co., 1991.

Steiner, Rudolf. *The Mission of the Folk Souls.* London: Rudolf Steiner Press, 1929.

Stevens, Dr. Anthony. *Archetypes: A Natural History of the Self.* New York: Quill, 1982.

Stewart, R. J. *Living Magical Arts: Imagination and Magic for the 21st Century.* London: Blandford, 1987.

———————— *Earth Light; The Ancient Path to Transformation: Rediscovering the Wisdom of Celtic & Faery Lore.* Shaftesbury, England: Element Books, 1992.

Swimme, Brian. *The Universe Is a Green Dragon.* Santa Fe: Bear & Co., l985.

Thich Nhat Hanh. *The Miracle of Mindfulness.* Boston: Beacon Press, l975.

Thompson, William Irwin, ed. *Gaia: A Way of Knowing, Implications of the New Biology.* Hudson, N. Y.: Lindisfarne Press, 1987.

Tomioka, Ariel. *On the Breath of the Gods.* Carmichael, Calif.: Helios House, 1988.

Van der Post, Laurens. *Jung and the Story of Our Time.* New York: Pantheon Books, 1976.

———————— *A Walk with a White Bushman.* New York: William Morrow & Co. Inc., 1986.

Vitvan. *Cosmology.* San Marcos: School of the Natural Order, 1951.

———————— *The Christos: Birth and Unfoldment.* Baker: School of the Natural Order, 1951.

Walsh, John E. *Intercultural Education in the Community of Man.* Honolulu: University of Hawaii Press, 1973.

Watts, Alan W. *Myth and Ritual in Christianity.* New York: Vanguard Press, 1953.

———————— *The Two Hands of God.* Collier Books, l963/69.

Wilbur, Ken. *No Boundary: Eastern and Western Approaches to Personal Growth.* Boston: Shambhala Publications, 1979.

Woodman, Marion. *Conscious Femininity.* Toronto: Inner City Books, 1993.